FILTH!

Compiled by Crispin Leyser
Devised by Ivor Dembina and Crispin Leyser

WRITTEN BY

Ben Elton, Julian Clary, Harry Enfield, Jo Brand, Eddie Izzard, Steve Coogan, Arthur Smith, Mark Lamarr, Lynn Ferguson, Greg Proops, Mark Thomas, Lily Savage, John Hegley, Rhona Cameron, Jeff Green, Trev and Simon, Mike McShane, Ian Cognito, Gayle Tuesday, Maureen Lipman, Jeremy Hardy, Absolutely, Sean Hughes, Simon Fanshawe, Spitting Image, Steve Punt, Sandi Toksvig, Mark Burton, John O'Farrell

PHOTOGRAPHS BY
Michael Le Poer Trench

CARTOONS BY

Will Kevans, Steve Best, Tony Husband, Noel Ford, Roland Fiddy, Steve Bell, Mike Flanagan, John Hegley

PROJECT COORDINATOR
Mark Higham

𝔸
ARROW

Arrow Books
in association with
The Terrence Higgins Trust

First published in 1994

1 3 5 7 9 10 8 6 4 2

©Terrence Higgins Enterprises 1994

First published in the United Kingdom in 1994 by Arrow,
Random House UK, 20 Vauxhall Bridge Road, London, SW1V 2SA

Random House Australia (Pty) Limited
20 Alfred Street, Milsons Point, Sydney
New South Wales 2061, Australia

Random House New Zealand Limited
18 Poland Road, Glenfield, Auckland 10,
New Zealand

Random House South Africa (Pty) Limited
PO Box 337, Bergvlei, South Africa

Random House UK Limited Reg. No. 954009

A CIP catalogue record for this book
is available from the British Library

ISBN 0 09 949061 7

Designed by
Roger Walker Studio/Linde Hardaker

Printed and bound in Great Britain by
Cox & Wyman Ltd, Reading, Berks

ACKNOWLEDGEMENTS

With thanks to…
Geoff Posner, Lesley Davies, Pozzitive TV,
Lee Green, Andrew Zein, IPH Westhall   Ltd,
Pickwick UK Ltd, Simon Vaughan, Elaine
Robertson, Duncan Abell, Sadler's Wells
Theatre, Time Out Magazine, Simon Buckley,
Nigel   Plaskitt,   John   Thirtle,   Barnaby
Harrison, Brian Herring, Patrick Comerfield,
Roger Blake, Jan Ravens, Rocco Redondo

CONTENTS

ERIC AND ERNIE
A Short Story by Arthur Smith

I think Tony was more than surprised when, at the end of the evening in Aghios Nikolas, I cut my little finger off. When I said to Tony, 'Will you give me £50 if I cut my finger off?', he naturally agreed. He didn't expect that within thirty seconds I would produce an electric carving knife and slice straight through halfway down the finger. He got a bit hysterical, actually, and once I'd attended to the blood, I had to slap him with my right hand. I explained that I was going to get £3,000 from the insurance company and I had planned it all along, but he still seemed shaken and left soon after. I never saw him again but, to be fair, he did send me the £50.

Now, that story is by way of explaining how it is that I come to have two penises. I am the sort of man who would do anything rather than work. You see, I met a rich man in a pub six months ago and he asked me about my missing finger. It turned out he was a cosmetic surgeon. The best cosmetic surgeon in London, he reckoned. He claimed that if he was paid enough, he could transform Raymond Baxter into Philip Schofield. To be honest, I didn't know who Raymond Baxter was, but I got the idea. He was bored with tooth-capping and lipo-suction, and he was really excited about some of the new ideas coming out of America. You can kind of guess the rest, I suppose. £20,000 he paid me. I didn't take it lightly. I made sure there was no real danger. The worst that could happen, he told me, was that my original penis might reject the new one. But, in that event, the new one would just wither away and he could cut if off painlessly. If it worked, then I would be the most extraordinary man in the world.

When I came round, my testicles really ached. They felt as though Boris Becker had been whacking them with a tennis racket solidly for several hours. My eyes were sore, too, because as cover for Dr Mike, I had also agreed to have a

► 1

face-lift and a nose-job. It was some time before all the bandages were off and I was finally able to pull the blanket up and have a good look at my new prick. It was rather unimpressive – skinny and red with stitches all round the stump. I felt a bit sorry for it, poor thing – it had had an eventful month. One moment, it was nestling happily in a pair of trousers on the M25, the next, it was being grafted onto an entirely new body. I had to stop this sort of thought. I didn't want to think about my new penis's previous history. It was important, as Dr Mike said, that I treat it as one of the family. He also suggested that I should not talk about 'the old one' and 'the new one'. So I decided to give them names. After some thought, I hit upon Morecambe and Wise – as I always thought they were really funny. Besides, the new one bore a passing resemblance to Eric Morecambe. I hoped, too, that when Eric began to feel at home he and Ernie might begin to work as a double act, if you see what I mean.

Not long after I came out of the clinic, I was able to piss through Morecambe and, not long after that, I woke to find Eric winking happily at me and sporting an erection. I jumped out of bed to look at it in the mirror and was alarmed at its unusual shape: the first half stuck straight out; the second made a sharp turn upwards so that it was parallel with my body. I had an L-shaped erection. In profile, in conjunction with the limp Ernie, I seemed to have the number '4' protruding from my abdomen. That night, Dr Mike gave me an injection. Next day, I woke up with aching balls and two erections. The effect was like some art-house comment on Winston Churchill. Eric seemed a little straighter, like a miniature crossbow. I tentatively embarked on a double wank. It was terribly hard to co-ordinate my hands. I was trying to wrist Eric slower than Ernie. Eventually, I found a decent rhythm and Ernie responded in the old-fashioned way and took a nose-dive. Turning my attentions to Eric, I suddenly felt both delirious and ecstatic as my fingers ran the banana curve of his outline. When he sent his creamy message, I was so

▶ 2

(TRANSLATION; 'FUCK ME SIDEWAYS, IT'S IN STEREO!')

exhausted that I forgot to smear the contents of the sheets on to the slide Dr Mike had given me. I fell into a deep sleep, and woke up and went to 'Kents'.

I used to go to Kents and pick up girls. I'm quite good at it actually. I look a bit like Bob Geldof with a bent nose – and I'm quite funny. Oddly, they really liked the half-a-little finger. One girl asked me to put it up her and wiggle it about. Matt, the barman, didn't recognise me at first and, when he heard my voice, he looked startled: 'What the fuck happened to your face?' 'I had a face-lift and a nose-job.' He looked bemused. 'And I've had a second penis grafted on.' At this, he burst out laughing. To his further amazement, I ordered champagne. I sat down to wait for some girls to arrive and considered my plan of attack. Surely, I reasoned to myself, having two penises would be attractive to many women – just like my little finger. But, then again, I had an absence of finger but a double helping of penis. To lose a part of your body does occur; to acquire an extra bit might seem abnormal. To have two noses or three eyes is certainly unattractive. I never heard of Cyclops getting off with anyone. But two pricks – there's a thought.

▶ 3

Two blondes walked into the bar, I guessed Danish au pairs. A lot of Scandinavian au pairs go to Kents. I bided my time as they ordered two beers and I tried to imagine how wide my two dicks could spread. Eventually, I sent a bottle of champagne over to them with a note saying 'Are you Finnish air hostesses?' They looked surprised when it arrived. You probably notice I'm good at surprising people. But they accepted, nodded and smiled at me. I walked over and asked 'Well, are you?' The one in jeans smiled and put out her hand. 'We are students from Norway. I am Oola and this is Hannah.' Hannah was wearing a black skirt. She had long legs, small tits under a white vest and, on her feet, an ugly pair of trainers. She was unimaginably gorgeous. I knew immediately I would have to target Oola. It's not necessary to record the manoeuvrings, chattings and night out that led, two weeks later, to Hannah sitting on my settee at midnight sipping brandy. I hadn't thus far managed to tell her about my unusual attribute. It's not something that slots easily into conversation. Perhaps my only opportunity had come when she remarked that I always wore baggy trousers.

'Shall we go to bed?' she said, leaping several pages in the script. Within minutes, she was beneath my duvet, looking eager. I was quite eager, too. I not only fancied Hannah – I rather liked her as well. As I stripped and got into bed, I executed an elegant pirouette that expertly obscured Morecambe and Wise. Hannah bent over and kissed me on the lips six times. I could taste her lipstick and, on the seventh, I kissed back a little longer and a little harder. She gave a little gasp. Then she gave a very big gasp. Then she was standing by the bed, pinning the duvet to her chest with her hand and staring at me naked on the bed. Her eyes went from my two penises to my two eyes and back again. On her face was more surprise than I've ever seen before. I realised in a flash that I was going to have to get used to that expression.
(To be continued – if I can be bothered or if a publisher offers me some money.)

celebrity
sex
secrets

Filth – the questionnaire

Greg Proops

Q *What is your favourite sexual position?*

A The Etruscan Lobster
— painful but satisfying.

Q *Who in the world would you most like to shag?*

A The state of Michigan.

Q *Have you shagged anyone taking part in 'Filth!'? If so, who, if not, who would you most like to?*

A Yes. The producer, so I could do the show.

Q *When was the last time you had sex?*

A Is this an offer?

Q *Where and when was the first time you had sex?*

A April 4th 1975, and again June 18th 1977.

Q *What is your favourite sexual fantasy?*

A Tying Baroness Thatcher and Ronald Reagan together with liquorice.

Q *Where is your most powerful erogenous zone?*

A Just South.

Q *Do you spit or swallow?*

A Excuse me?

Q *Where do you most like to have sex?*

A Earth and it's satellite.

Q *Where is the most unusual place you've ever had sex?*

A The Gents' toilet in the House of Lords.

Filth – the questionnaire

Jo Brand

Q *What is your favourite sexual position?*

A Lying down, but that's my favourite position generally

Q *Who in the world would you most like to shag?*

A Walter Matthau

Q *Have you shagged anyone taking part in 'Filth!'? If so, who, if not, who would you most like to?*

A Yes, all of them

Q *When was the last time you had sex?*

A 1847

Q *Where and when was the first time you had sex?*

A During the french revolution

Q *What is your favourite sexual fantasy?*

A It involves Captain Von Trapp and the nuns in The Sound of Music

Q *Where is your most powerful erogenous zone?*

A Lost in France

Q *Do you spit or swallow?*

A Spit or swallow what? My dinner? Swallow

Q *Where do you most like to have sex?*

A In a nuclear reprocessing plant

Q *Where is the most unusual place you've ever had sex?*

A In a bed

Filth – the questionnaire

Mark Thomas

Q *What is your favourite sexual position?*

A Doggy style!

Q *Who in the world would you most like to shag?*

A Germaine Greer.

Q *Have you shagged anyone taking part in 'Filth!'? If so, who, if not, who would you most like to?*

A Greg Proops, to see if he giggles.

Q *When was the last time you had sex?*

A Today (ask Greg).

Q *Where and when was the first time you had sex?*

A In an alleyway behind a cinema, after watching a Woody Allen movie.

Q *What is your favourite sexual fantasy?*

A Being taken out to diner afterwards.

Q *Where is your most powerful erogenous zone?*

A All of me.

Q *Do you spit or swallow?*

A Gargle.

Q *Where do you most like to have sex?*

A Peter Lilley's office.

Q *Where is the most unusual place you've ever had sex?*

A In a squash court — in a sweet shop.

Filth – the questionnaire

Arthur Smith

Q *What is your favourite sexual position?*

A Sideways and turn second left at the roundabout.

Q *Who in the world would you most like to shag?*

A Valerie Singleton.

Q *Have you shagged anyone taking part in 'Filth!'? If so, who, if not, who would you most like to?*

A The front of house staff.

Q *When was the last time you had sex?*

A Clearly I'm writing this some weeks before the gig tonight. So I'll be optimistic and say 10 minutes ago.

Q *Where and when was the first time you had sex?*

A 1971 — with a bus stop.

Q *What is your favourite sexual fantasy?*

A Its fantastic.

Q *Where is your most powerful erogenous zone?*

A Birmingham.

Q *Do you spit or swallow?*

A I gargle then whistle.

Q *Where do you most like to have sex?*

A On Mother Kelly's Doorstep. down Paradise Way.

Q *Where is the most unusual place you've ever had sex?*

A This is true; the centre spot at Stamford Bridge (Chelsea Football Ground). Honest.

Filth – the questionnaire

Lynn Ferguson

Q *What is your favourite sexual position?*
A With a bloke.

Q *Who in the world would you most like to shag?*
A A bloke.

Q *Have you shagged anyone taking part in 'Filth!'? If so, who, if not, who would you most like to?*
A No.
Val Doonican.

Q *When was the last time you had sex?*
A Fortunately I've got Alzheimers.

Q *Where and when was the first time you had sex?*
A Watching Val Doonican singing 'Little Green Apples' on TV.

Q *What is your favourite sexual fantasy?*
A

Watching Val Doonican singing 'Little Green Apples' on TV.

Q *Where is your most powerful erogenous zone?*
A

My fanny

Q *Do you spit or swallow?*
A

Swallow first then spit.

Q *Where do you most like to have sex?*
A

Anywhere other than Coventry.

Q *Where is the most unusual place you've ever had sex?*
A

A pulpit in Dundee.

oral
sex

'WELL I'M AFRAID YOUR FEMINIST FRIEND WAS MISINFORMED ABOUT WHAT "ORAL SEX" MEANS.'

LILY SAVAGE

LILY SAVAGE

We all got one of these through the post, it's a questionnaire. [*reads off questionnaire*] 'What is your favourite sexual position?' I couldn't fucking believe this. This and the *Reader's Digest* came on Monday morning. 'Can you remember the first time you had sex?' I can't fucking remember the last, to tell you the truth. 'Do you spit or swallow?' What kind of question is that to ask anyone? What kind of filth is that, 'Do you spit?' I think oral sex is the most disgusting thing in the world! Men's dicks, err...my... Them little fat ones full of veins like a pensioner's leg, you think I'm going to put one of them in my gob, you've got another fucking think coming. Well, not for less than fifty quid anyway.

I don't know what God was thinking about when he made the reproductive organs, because the woman's isn't much better. It looks like a tomcat with its throat cut, have you seen it? And them balls hanging like two used teabags swinging off your chin. It's so fucking uncomfortable, lying there with two big hairy thighs either side of your face. You can't even get your gob open, you're like a goldfish. You're blowing air instead of sucking.

As for coming in the mouth [*muttered*], you know what I mean. It's like a vitamin E capsule exploding. Only ever done it once and that was by mistake. Sat on the bed, you're turning green, the sweat's running off you like a glass blower's arse. And he's taking ages getting dressed, smiling at you. 'Would you like a cup of coffee?' You go 'Mmm mm', which means 'Fuck off so I can spit this out.' And then they get fruity and want to kiss you again— 'Mmm mm', pull the headboard down [*spits*], get out and walk!

JEREMY HARDY

'John Patten, Eraserhead, he looks physically sick when he has to say the words 'sex education.' And he was appalled by that nurse in Leeds. This poor nurse in Leeds had to explain blow jobs and Mars Bar parties to some 10-year-olds; and some-body suggested that when a boy asked 'Miss, what is a blow job?', she should have taken the boy to one side and explained it to him. But you can't give that one boy the power of being the one kid who knows what it is. All the other kids would have been around him at play-time going,

'Oh go on, Colin, what is it?'

'I'm not telling you.'

'Oh, go on.'

'OK, I'll tell you...if you suck my knob.'

And the Mars Bar parties thing foxed me. I mean, I know about the apocryphal Marianne Faithful story and that obviously the origins of the practice of combining food with cunnilingus is that for a lot of women the only way they can get their man to do it is to put his dinner up there. You know, he comes home reeling drunk, missed his dinner; and there's an angry note on the table in the kitchen, 'Dinner's in me', and she's spread out on the table.

'ER...SORRY EVERYONE, I COULD ONLY GET KIT KATS.'

I just wouldn't have thought a Mars Bar would go; I would have thought maybe some steamed vegetables, or a salad possibly.

But Mars Bar parties I was a bit worried about...I think guests are entitled to a plate, call me old-fashioned. And if you go to a Mars Bar party do you have to have a Mars Bar? Can you have a Twix or some crudités or something?

But the nurse said she was very careful to explain this within the context of a loving relationship. But you don't do things like that in the context of a loving relationship; you go to Ikea within the context of a loving relationship. You do things with Mars Bars in the context of a brief fling with some mad dirty bastard that you have to break up with because they're doing your head in.

MARK THOMAS

Did you know that they'd invented this thing called the Dental Dam, for safe oral sex between heterosexuals? What it is, is a piece of latex, and it goes over the woman's genitals. We call it the picnic cloth in our house, it's very sweet. Now I don't know if you can get the HIV virus from oral sex, but if you can, and if the virus actually wants to connect, it had better be fucking quick. It would have to be. Because some boys are like [*takes one lick*], 'Done that. Your turn now.'

And boys get reticent about going down, because sometimes when you're going down, you can be right there, you can be right on the bingo button, the fleshy pearl of joy, on the magic spot, and suddenly you get images of your family cropping up in your subconscious. So you're down there, and suddenly your mum and dad appear. 'Get your elbows off the table while you're eating! Don't slurp, don't use your fingers.' If I have kids, I'm going to be there at the dinner table, 'Just lick that fucking plate, come on! Lick it! Come on. Give me that butter dish... something furry, kiwi fruit. See, not frightening. That's good, isn't it?'

Because...I don't think children should grow up with sexual taboos. If I have a son and he's heterosexual and he says, 'Dad, I'm going out tonight on a date', I'll say,
'Alright, son, but what are the three golden rules?'
'Oh, er, lead in slowly with the long strokes, always stimulate the clitoris, and, er...',
'Come on, son...',
'And, er, a gentleman always goes down first.'
'That's right, son. Now, I think your mother wants a quick word about nipple stimulation.'

continued...

MARK THOMMAS

And while we're on the subject, the trouble with cunnilingus, the trouble...First of all, getting there. Because you've got those luscious, lovely, labby lips, and getting there is like flicking through the paper. 'Where the fucking hell is it?' I want a big bookmark, a big bookmark by the clit...No, a fridge magnet, a fridge magnet on it, which says 'clit' in dayglo letters. But if you hit the button, there should be a scout badge for that; just a little triangle with a golden tongue.

I'll leave you with this; this is my idea of a moral dilemma: most blokes, at some stage of their life, have tried to give themselves a blow job. There's a lot of denial going on in the room, isn't there? There's probably a few couples going, 'Did you?'
'No I fucking did not.'
'Did you try...?'
'No I did not...'
'Come here, let me smell your breath.'
'No, fuck off!'
The moral dilemma here isn't that you tried. The moral dilemma is if you could actually do it. There's the dilemma. Do you make yourself swallow? What do you do? Half of you is going, 'Suck it, suck it, like the bitch that you are, suck it good.' And the other half's going, 'Fucking hell, it's going to come out my nose.' Do you tell your friends, do you tell your relatives? Do they regard it as a gift? Every Christmas when the family gather round, 'Mark, show them what you can do.'

EDDIE IZZARD

On a lighter note, today is National Oral Sex day, as you all know. There was a march today down Whitehall; everyone marching down, saying, 'What do we want?!' 'Omumum.' [*Mumbles as if mouth was full of come.*] 'And how we gonna get it?!' [*Cough, splutter*].

RHONA CAMERON

'Do you know what audiences do if they get really nasty in this country? If there's someone on the stage, they just use one word to show their disapproval, don't they? Just one classic word. 'Booooooooo!' I went to the Royal Opera and there was this heckler who went 'Booooo!' and everyone went, 'Booooo! It's an outrage!' Politicians use it, too. If they disagree with something, they just say, 'Excuse me. Booooooo!' Sometimes comics go, 'I had a fucking dreadful night last night, I got booed off.' 'Surely not boo?' 'Yes, I'm afraid so.' 'Not "bollocks"?' 'No, just boo.' It's terrible. But imagine if you went home with someone and you had sex with them for the first time and it was shit, imagine if when they were going down on you, you just went, 'Booooo! Boo! Get off, you're terrible! Boo!' That would actually be the ultimate humiliation, to be booed off someone's vagina onto the street.'

BESTIE

'JUST A KISS WILL DO HARDY!'

swearwords
and **language**

MARK THOMAS

Good news, good news. From now on there's going to be a whole fucking bucket-load of swearing, that's the good news from me. Fucking bundles, because I fucking love swearing. And I think it's really clever as well, OK? I think it's really fucking intelligent. Because if you look at what we are, all we are is carbon and calcium and H_2O. We're just chemical vessels. Vessels of stupidity, greed, inanity, jealousy, envy, lust...But why bother with all that when you've got a word like 'wanker'? Why bother? Beautiful word.

I like swearing because my family swore more than anyone else I know in the world. If there was an Olympics for swearing, my mum and dad would be there representing Britain. My dad would be there doing the fuck puck, 'FUCKAAAH'. My mum would be there doing the gymnastics, 'arsehole-bastard-shit-arse-fuck-arsehole-shit-fuck'. My nan swore more than anyone else in the world, and she was deaf. So someone would leave the room and you'd hear, 'He's a bit of a shit-gobbler isn't he?' And we're standing on the doorstep saying, 'Thanks for coming, Doctor, really appreciate that, it's really kind of you.' 'Cold fingers! No wonder I fucking spasmed!' 'She didn't, she's fine, she's fine.'

I knew every single swearword when I was seven. Didn't know what they meant, but I knew them. When I was seven, I actually knew the phrase, 'muff-diver'. True; because my dad used it before a seven-year-old at the breakfast table. And his exact words were: 'Son, never go muff-diving before breakfast, you get all the hairs in your...yaaaaa.' And I heard the phrase 'muff-diving' and I thought, interesting words. And then I heard my mum go, 'Colin!' and I thought, good words. I love swearing; my favourite swearwords are 'fuck', because that's like the Swiss Army Penknife of swearing. You can use it for anything. It's brilliant: 'You fucked it, you fucker, fuck it, we'll get another, fucking great'. Lovely, that's brilliant.

'Wank'. What a wonderful word 'wank' is, because it's got a 'wa' and a 'ka' and I'm easily pleased.

My favourite word of the whole lot isn't strictly speaking a swearword, though; my favourite word is 'clit'. What a fantastic word. And I love the accordion version of 'clit-or-is', [*smacks his lips*]. Just say it, 'clitoris', just saying it encourages cunnilingus. 'Clitoris, clitoris.' Just go down and say it 400 times really quick, OK? 'Clitoris', it's a great word. There should be a Shakespeare character called 'Clitoris'. 'What ho, my noble Lord of Clit', 'Well met, my Duke of Vulva.' Fantastic word, 'clitoris'. We've had the Montego, we've had the Capri, I want the 'Clitoris'. A small car, good on petrol, easy to park, bit of a fucker to find once you've left it...rummaging round the car park for half an hour.

The other reason that I love swearing is because there are some things that you can't say unless you swear. You can't talk about whole subjects, unless you swear. 'Peter Fucking Lilley', can't be done, I've tried it.

ARTHUR SMITH

I like Americans, although I sometimes had a bit of trouble with the language when I went to America. For example, what we call trousers, Americans call pants; and what we call braces, American call suspenders. So, this guy invited me to a party. He said: 'Hey, Arthur, wanna go to a party?' I said, 'Yeah, what shall I wear?' and he said, 'Well, I should wear pants and suspenders.' So I did. Best bloody party I've ever been to, absolutely brilliant affair.

LYNN FERGUSON

Do you get upset if I say cunt? I say cunt sometimes down here and people get upset. I have to explain to them that in

Scotland cunt is a compliment, it is. If you like somebody you go 'You're a good cunt'. If you come home with a good report card, your mum will go 'fucking smart cunt, you'.

Brother Trevor

Brother Trevor handed in his cowl
and his trowel
and took leave of his order for ever,
taking a position as a warder
in an already overcrowded prison.
And after the celibate years
being thought of as 'a screw'
took a bit of getting used to.

John Hegley

RHONA CAMERON

If you're a woman and you go on holiday, you do have to endure a certain amount of dreadful chat-up from men abroad. It's pretty bad here, but in some places like Spain, there are some men who learn six or seven words in English, and think that if they just repeat them to you (it doesn't have to be in the right order or interesting or anything), that they'll get a fucking shag. Like when strangers come up to you in the street, they'll say to me, 'Oh you come from Edinburgh, there's a festival, that's interesting, isn't it?' 'Yes, fucking great.' So, I went to Majorca (I'm working class), to get a tan. And I was sitting there by the sea, reading, which is a clear indication that I don't want to talk to anyone. And this Spanish man came up to me, with a very original introductory chat-up line. He just says, 'You like to read?' I said, 'Yes, I do like to read and I come from Edinburgh and there's a festival. So fuck off.' And he's still there trying to bore the tits off me and this time he goes, 'Aha, the sea is good?' So I thought, I'm just going to teach him the most offensive words completely out of context, because he can't understand anything I'm saying. So I just smiled like a girly and said, 'No, it's a bit cuntish, actually. Yes, that's right, lots of labia around your head today.' I also told him that 'Minging Pish Flaps' was a really friendly expression.

PAUL CALF

I'm not scared to talk about sex. I'll say, 'Cunnilingus'. I'll fucking shout it. 'CUNNILINGUS!' I don't know what it fucking means.

IAN COGNITO

I just want to say the reason I'm doing this gig is because there's no censorship involved, they're not going to censor anything we say, which is brilliant, 'cause I hate censorship. Because I was arguing with my next-door neighbour the other day, 'cause I'm from Walthamstow and he was a Muslim geezer, yes, multi-cultural Walthamstow—I live next door to some Muslim people, upstairs we've got African people, next door I've got Greek orthodox people and we all get on very well, thanks very much for asking...'Cause we all gang up on the Eskimos down the bottom of the fucking garden. Any Eskis in tonight? Fucking wankers, they are. Do you know your Eskimo lives in the coldest part of the world, and what do they make their house out of? Ice—now that's just stupid. They've got 147 words for snow and not one for cunnilingus...Mind you, be fair, if you spent all your days covered in fur and smelling of fish, you can have too much of a good thing. So, I'm arguing with my next-door neighbour and I say, 'What you have done to Salman

Rushdie is out of order, this is supposed to be a free country.' (Mind you, speaking of Salman Rushdie, have you lot noticed how we've seen a lot more of him since he went into hiding; now that's fucking weird, isn't it? Because until he started hiding I didn't know what the cunt looked like. Not a very good hider, is he? And I use the word cunt, because I think it's about time you women stopped using our swearwords for your private parts; they're our swearwords.) So, I said, 'Listen mate, what you've done to Salman Rushdie is out of order...' He said, 'Alright mate, but here's an interesting point for you; do you know that if you rearrange the letters of Salman Rushdie you come up with "Al Slurman dies"?' So, I said, 'Well two can play at that game, 'cause if you rearrange the letters of Nigel Mansell, you come up with 'a line of smeg'; or rearrange the letters of Cecil Parkinson, you get 'ol' penis in crack'; Kylie Minogue—'you like minge'. Bill Clinton—'nob in clit'; Kate Adie—'eat a dike' (don't blame me, I never called her Kate); and now we've got a Health Minister called Virginia Bottomley. I mean, if your name was Virginia would you marry someone called Bottomley?— No. Mind you, it's not a widely known fact that Virginia's maiden name was Cuntington.

JEFF GREEN

They do this a lot in London, don't they?

You've got to call every cyclist you see a wanker. That's a weird thing, isn't it? They can't just call you wanker, they've got to give the mime as well for wanker; in case you don't know what one is...

'Wanker.'

'What? Oh right, yes, that'll be me you're talking about.'
   'Cause you've been doing...

...that all your life.

They're just helping you out.
   'Do that.'

'I've been doing this.'

'You're a fool, that's...

...better.'
'Thanks for the tip, I can't wait to get home. There's a bus shelter there, I'm going to pull over and try.'

'Cause blokes are terrible, they do it all the time to each other.
'Hey you, Wanker!'

I wonder, do women ever go back...

'Wanker.'

Do you? You should do, shouldn't you?
Am I doing that...

...right, by the way? It's very difficult, isn't it?

Sketch starring TREV as Scout Leader, Monty Powell, **& SIMON** as Woody Hibbard...

SL: Come on, be quiet everybody and listen to me. Let us introduce ourselves. I'm Scout Leader, Monty Powell, and this is my assistant here, Woody Hibbard.

WH: Hello, I'm Woody Hibbard, assistant to Scout Leader...

SL: Yes, alright, alright, I've done all that, we've not got much time. Now of course everything tonight has been done for charity, and there's nothing wrong with that, but frankly, I'm appalled by some of the material I've heard so far.

WH: Yes, we're not impressed, are we Scout Leader? We're not impressed by all these silly jokes about sexual behaviour.

SL: No we're not. There's nothing funny about sex. We've all done it.

WH: Well, actually, I haven't, Scout Leader.

SL: No, but you've seen me do it. Now we can all giggle about sex. Now what I say is: get on with it, get it over with and put it back in your pants where it belongs.

WH: Yes, OK. Now while we're here we'll thank you to refrain from making silly remarks aimed at people like ourselves, so we'll have no giggling at our woggles, and no sniggering at our ging-gang-goolies, OK? It's a tradition that goes back many years, and you must remember that goolies didn't mean then what it means now.

SL: No, but bollocks did. Oh yes, bollocks, testicles, nuts, say what you see.

WH: Yes, OK, Scout Leader. Now I've been involved with the Boy Scout movement all my life. I couldn't wait to be a Boy Scout, so I got straight into the Beavers.

SL: Where would we be without those little beavers?

WH: Indeed, but you must remember that beaver didn't mean then what it means now.

SL: No, but fanny did. Keep your hands out of the beds, boys! Oh yes, dib dib dib, dob dob dob, keep your hands off your nob!

WH: The fundraising, yes. Charity. Well, what we're going to do, we're going to give all the proceeds from our Annual bob-a-job week.

WH: Now for those of you who don't remember, bob-a-job week was when Scouts and Cubs would go out and do little jobs for people, and they'd be rewarded with a bob or a shilling.

SL: Yes, now of course, these days, a shilling is 5p and a bob, well bob is just the name of a man, isn't it?

WH: Well, that brings us on to our plan for bob-a-job week. Yes, we're going to get all the famous Bobs, like Bob Monkhouse and Bob Hope...

VOICE OFFSTAGE: Bob Carolgees

SL: Yes, we can all think of a few famous Bobs.

WH: So, Bob Monkhouse could maybe mow somebody's lawn, or Bob Hope could clean somebody's windows.

SL: Yes, well, maybe they could, but that's not what we're planning. No, we want these famous Bobs to do a job. Yes, that's right, to do their business, to do a jobby! Do a number two!

WH: That's right, then we're going to auction them to raise the money, so...we want to encourage all the famous Bobs to do a dump or a plop plop and then all the donated stools will be collected by members of the Scout movement.

SL: Yes, and that's how we got our motto: 'A movement for the movement!'

WH   Although 'movement' didn't mean then what it means now.

SL: No, but big fat stinking turd did!

WH: Alright, Scout Leader, yes.

SL: Now, perhaps you could look at some of the examples that we've already got.

[*WH removes jar from bag in which is a turd*]

WH: We've got a very special donation here from a very famous Bob. Yes, this is from Sir Bob Geldof. There we go.

[*WH unscrews top of jar*]

SL: Oh yes, see. Oh, you can tell he's a vegetarian, can't you?

WH: And legendary folk singer Bob Dylan has also sent us a piece of his own excrement...Yes, a Travelling Wilberries LP.

SL: Of course, that gives you the idea of the thing, but now let's get on with a bit of entertainment.

WH: OK. We're going to sing you a song now from the old original Scout songbook from 1954.

SL: Yes now, it bemuses me a bit, but it seems some of you find our old gang shows and some of the songs we sing in them faintly amusing.

WH: Yes, I don't know why. What on earth is wrong with good old songs like this—I'll go down the list: 'Heave Away My Johnny', and 'Bobby Shaftoe', and other traditional scouting songs like 'Donkey Riding', 'Blow Pipers Blow' and my particular favourite, 'Come Landlord Fill the Flowing Bowl'. Yes, all very funny, but you must remember, 'come' didn't mean then what it means now.

SL: No no, but spunk did!

TREV & SIMON

WH: OK, alright.

SL: Happy cream! Talking, talking, talking, happy cream...

WH: Scout Leader, shall we sing now? We're going to sing an old favourite. It's all about road safety and zebra crossings and it's got no rude meanings in it whatsoever, and it's called 'Carry A Little Belisha Beacon Everywhere You Go'. Have you got the beacons, Scout Leader?

SL: Yes, I've got them over here.

[*SL fetches hand-held Belisha beacons which flash on and off*]

WH: I'll just tune up on the piano then.

SL: Here we are. Now would you like to take yours, Woody? And now we'll sing, ladies and gentleman... Oh, look Woody, look, my end is flashing.

WH: Careful, Scout Leader, remember 'my end is flashing' didn't mean then what it means now.
SL: No, but throbbing penis did!

WH: OK! Let's just sing, shall we, Scout Leader? I'm ready, Scout Leader.

[*They sing*]

Carry a little Belisha Beacon everywhere you go,
When you hold your beacon up, the traffic goes so slow;
It really is amazing how the traffic does respond
When you walk along with your little magic wand.
In the afternoon if you should go out for a stroll
Don't forget to take your little bladder on a pole;
Greta Garbo with a moan says you'll never be alone,
When you've got your little beacon in your hand.

SHE COMES FIRST
A Short Story by Mike McShane

In the spring of 1988 I began part-time work in an animal
shelter. Not out of any sense of kinship with the beasts: I had
to work off a number of parking tickets and after a disastrous
affair with a harpist in the local symphony, my fingers and
self-worth were lacerated beyond repair. I wanted to forget,
and this seemed like the next best thing to the Foreign Legion,
and I could drive there.

The animal shelter was located in the desolate part of town
that used to be the railroad and shipping district. It was a large
warehouse, and, like many institutions whose sole purpose is
to bring solace and comfort to the unfortunate, it was under-
staffed, underfunded and largely ignored except for the occasional charity event, which in this case was an excuse for
concerned socialites to dress up and act like animals and save
them at the same time. My first job then was to clean up after
such an event, whose theme was 'The Thumping Party Island
of Dr Moreau'. No little irony was lost on me as I cleaned up
behind my fellow species, only to find that, in the time evolution has given us acute eyesight and the opposable thumb, we
still manage to miss the toilet, and confuse it with the sink.
The animals that actually resided there were confined to the
back. There were no domestic pets, though: those were at
another shelter. This was reserved for the wildlife that lived
and sadly sometimes died in the city: raccoons, owls, hawks
and foxes: denizens living a braver and far more dangerous
urban life than any black-clad art school devotee could imagine in their wildest dreams.

As you can see, I had become a Class-A misanthrope, taking
no delight in man, and so it had struck me as extremely cruel
that the only human being that I had to deal with at the shelter
was the most chirpy, platitude-spewing product of alternative
thinking that California ever vomited onto its shores. His

name was Tarpin, and he practised breathing exercises continually and wore a large block of camphor around his neck. The noise of his breathing frightened the animals out of their wits, and it was my fervent hope that someday, if he stopped his breathing exercises, his involuntary muscle system wouldn't kick in, and he would die.

One afternoon I loped into the shelter to work off some hours, and Tarpin was puttering around the back, talking and wheezing to the animals. He turned and greeted me with the memorable line, 'How goes the Voyage, my brother?' I grunted back to him, having by this point regressed to a near simian state to avoid talking to him. I walked over to the broom closet, grabbed a wet mop and proceeded cleaning in front of the cages. It was the end of the week and most of the animals had been returned to some form of the wild, except for a brown fox who had developed respiratory problems. At first I thought it was only imitating Tarpin to irritate him, but then I realised that even a fox would soon tire of taunting an idiot such as Tarpin, or it would be in danger of losing its cunning status. After I finished the floors, I was about to start on the cage that belonged to the fox, but Tarpin stopped me and said he had a special treat to show me. He started dancing around, wheezing harder and harder, and told me that foxes of course need prey as well as regular food for their diet, and he had got something at the farmers' market. It was then I realised what a twisted pig Tarpin was. So between Tarpin and the fox's expectant wheezing I was slowly going brainwhip and had reached meringue-like consistency when he brought his prize into the room.

It was a large, white chicken, and I would have thought it already dead if I hadn't seen it blinking. It hung there as if it were conscious of being sacrificed, and had given up all hope. I felt a deep sympathy for the chicken and tried to negotiate with Tarpin. 'Look,' I said, 'isn't there a smaller, less messy animal we can feed the fox? I certainly wouldn't want to clean up after it.' Tarpin moved away from the fox's cage and looked at me, hurt and distressed. 'You don't understand. I hate chickens!' I thought that misplaced envy might be a more suitable emotion for him, but I went on, patronising him as best I could. 'Tarpin, maybe you should analyse and identify the source of your feelings, instead of acting rashly, and perhaps regretfully.' I had barely finished what I was saying when the problem was removed from both our hands. Tarpin had already removed the catch from the cage, and suddenly the fox leapt out and onto Tarpin's head, exacting his revenge for centuries of blood sport.

Immediately, I did the only humane thing possible. I kicked Tarpin in the balls and grabbed the chicken. The fox didn't so much as break his stride when I did this: he must have hated Tarpin as much as I did. I ran out the back door with the chicken. I was in a state of utter panic, trying to come up with an idea of what to do with this chicken. That's when I noticed that the chicken was still, so very still and calm. I looked at the chicken; it looked at me and said in a distinctly sultry voice, 'Thank you for saving my life. Take me home, darling.' I fainted on the spot.

It was dusk when I awoke in my own house. Surely it had been a dream, but when I looked over to the kitchen and saw the chicken sitting on a bar stool mixing drinks, and swaying softly to a Bonnie Raitt song, I concluded I'd gone over the edge. I sat up and said, 'How did I get here?' She explained calmly that she drove me home in my car. I ran outside and checked. The car was there, and the front seat had been pushed very far forward, and a stack of overdue library books I'd been meaning to return had been placed on the accelerator. Numbly, I walked back into the apartment.

When I came through the door she was waiting for me, drinks in hand. 'Maybe we should just relax a little and get to know each other.' The idea shocked me. I really don't like talking about myself, and what would I say? But she moved so elegantly, so seductively, carrying the martinis over without spilling a drop, that I found myself sitting on the bed chatting away happily. The martini was superb, the old way, the Sinatra way. I finished it quickly. It must have gone straight to my head, for suddenly I was dizzy and had a splitting headache. She told me to lie back and she would take care of it for me. She climbed up on the bed and nestled very snugly on my forehead. She told me to close my eyes. I obeyed, and suddenly I was flooded with this incredible warmth, a soft, downy comfort that leeched my headache away until it was but a memory. When I opened my eyes I sat her next to me. I was grateful, intrigued and, may I say it, a little excited.

I proceeded to spend the most glorious evening of my life, asking her all kinds of questions, and listening raptly to her life story. She was born outside Petaluma and was one of the first 'free-range' chickens, originally a political movement which had been reduced to crass commercialism in order to survive. After that she had participated in a number of resistance groups, all failed. She said it was very difficult to organise animals with such a short attention span. I was puzzled. I said, 'What is it that makes you so different?' It was hard not to place too emotional a weight on that last word. She knew, and fanned me coquettishly with her wing and proceeded to explain that she was an anomaly, a lone leap forward in evolution. Upon learning how to speak, she had demanded an explanation from the farmer who raised her. It tragically resulted in the poor man having a heart attack. From that point on she had borne her awful burden in silence. Until now. I felt humbled by her trust, and unworthy.

I asked her to go on. She unfolded an amazing story of the history of poultry and mankind, our inexorable link through time and the great respect that primitive agrarian societies placed upon the chicken. She mentioned sadly that the Venus of Willendorf actually began as a tribute to a full-breasted and plump-thighed hen, complete with beak and tail feathers, now lost to history or destroyed by spiteful looters.

She finished, and there was a long and heavy silence between us. It was late, but I wasn't sleepy: in fact I would have gladly gone on listening to her, sitting at the edge of my bed, admiring her, wanting her. She knew, and after a moment said, 'I must be leaving you tomorrow.' I jumped up and protested, pacing the room feverishly. 'You don't have to,' I said. 'Why? I mean, you could stay here. No one would know. I could build you a nest in the corner of the room.' She smiled and said shyly, 'I'd much rather sleep with you. Let's just have tonight together.' She pulled back the sheets and the faint moonlight illuminated her. And with gratitude and tender hands I caressed and held her, making her tremble with pleasure as man and chicken must have done centuries ago, when we were one.

She was magnificent, so yielding and so passionate that I know that no other woman could satisfy me now. She had spoiled me, and I held her so she might never go away. And for the first time in months I slept deeply and well.

I awoke around noon the next day and she was not with me. I searched around and under the bed. Had she left, I wondered? I arose and continued to search, growing more frantic as I worked my way through the hallway and became fearful as I came into the kitchen. There on the floor in front of the stove was a neat pile of feathers and on the stove a large pot of boiling water. Next to it was a note. 'My Beloved, I told you I must leave today and I must. Each chicken has its time on earth and must move on. I know that after last night, everything else would pale to insignificance and I would want you night and day, and never share you with anyone. And one thing a chicken is not is selfish. Anyway darling, I would only bring suspicion and embarrassment to you. How would you explain me to your friends, your family? This world is not ready to come to grips with interspecies romance: I doubt it ever will be. I started the water. I'm in the refrigerator. Do what you must. You've had me every way, have me once more. I love you.'

I cried. I cried as I cut the onions, I cried as I cut the celery: and as I dressed her I wept, shaking, railing against the heavens. Such injustice. Then it was over. She was done. The noodles were *al dente* and my heart once again was broken. Don't ask me what heartache and loss feel like. I don't know what they feel like. But I know what they taste like. They taste a lot like chicken.

sex
symbols

WHILE SINGING IN THE HILLS MARIA SUDDENLY REALISED SHE DIDN'T WANT TO BE A NUN AFTER ALL

Princess Diana

Well I saw her first in a magazine
at the Doctor's, in *The Horse and Hound*,
Or was it *Harpers & Queen*?
She's the kind of girl I wouldn't talk to in a million years,
And even if I did she'd confirm all my fears,
Well, what's her name and what's her game?
Tell me, what's her claim to fame...?
Oh, Princess Diana, she's Princess Diana,

We could have a really groovy time together,
Now that she's finally rid of that big-eared fella (1)
She's surrounded by photographers all of the time,
And I'm just trying to work out a way to get into her pants...
Or get her into mine.
Though she's 30, she's still flirty,
Me and her could get quite dirty,
She looks so cute in her tracksuit,
She's the only royal I really want to root, (2)
Oh, Diana, we're really going to miss you.

Well I never fancied old ginger minge,
Although I'm too much of a gentleman to say,
I'd take a run at Prince Edward but
He just won't admit that he's gay.
Princess Anne just can't compare with the fair Diana,
She makes my nuts tighten up, I call her Princess Spanner. (3)
Diana, she's Princess Diana.

(1) Although, fair play to Charlie, they took a couple of shots at him in Australia and he didn't flinch...told you he was fucking stupid didn't I?

(2) Although...a couple of tabs of E and I've even toyed with the idea of going down on the Queen Mother. Don't pretend that you haven't.

(3) That's why I'm in the comedy business, lines like that. With lines as good as that you don't need a widget.

Ian Cognito

BEN ELTON

‘We are constantly led to believe by the magazines that we are simply inadequate. You see the supermodels and you think that no one could ever look like that. Those women are eight feet tall, they're teetering along the catwalk. Extraordinary—tits on the ceiling, shoes on the floor, nothing in the middle.

And every one married to a farty little rock star. You've got these incredibly long women and this farty little rock star on her hand. Incredibly tall woman, farty little rock star waddling beside her. Mick Jagger, Simon Le Bon, David Bowie, that bloke out of U2—incredibly tall wife, farty little rock star. He's saying, 'I may not have had a hit since 1979, but I've fucked her, alright?'

There is snow on the peak, know what I mean? I mean, these women, they are anorexic. When I see them on the catwalk in Paris or Milan, I keep expecting the UN to fly in food, or Michael Burke to jump up and say, 'These women are literally starving.' You see them all with their farty little rock stars, incredibly tall woman, a farty little rock star. When they all go out together at Planet Hollywood or something like that, it reminds me of that bit in Mickey Mouse's *Fantasia*, where all the mops dance with the buckets.

I mean how could a real woman achieve that figure? You just can't do it. The only way you could look like that would be if you went down the fairground. The fairground mirrors, isn't that a laugh? 'Oo, look, the tits up there, the shoes down there, aren't I a laugh, hey?' Don't stand there laughing too long or Mick Jagger will come up behind you and shag you!'

Man and Gran United

Grandma she was walking
with her dog by the canal
when she recognised a foreign man
who wasn't an Italian,
it was Eric Cantona
he was sitting on a bench
Eric is a football star
and Eric's French.
Eric Cantona, Eric Cantona
he likes to kick the ball under the bar
Eric Cantona, Eric Cantona
Grandma's favourite footballer by far.
The dog jumped up on Eric's bench
and Eric said *bonjour*,
the doggie made an awful stench
and Eric he said eughh
(but he said it in French).
Grandma said I'm sorry Eric
Eric said *c'est la vie*
and Grandma thought he said celery.
Then Eric spoke in English
and asked the doggie's name
and Grandma said I call him Jesus
because he isn't just for Christmas.
Then doggie fouled the pavement
and Eric fouled the dog.
Eric Cantona, Eric Cantona
Gerard Depardieu it isn't who you are.
Eric Cantona, Eric Cantona
a banana with no ner is a bana.

John Hegley

GAYLE TUESDAY

LYNN FERGUSON

I was asked to be a bit sexy and dirty; and I said well, you know, it's fucking difficult for me, because I am Scottish...and Scottish people aren't very sexy, are they? I was trying to think of good Scottish sex symbols and people always say Sean Connery; but am I right or am I a meringue...is he just a baldy pensioner with a moustache—and a speech impediment?

And the other favourite that people always say is Robert Burns; great poet and all that...and would have shagged an open wound.

The other favourite is Bonny Prince Charlie; his real name was Charles Edward Stuart, but he was nicknamed Bonny Prince Charlie because he was 4'9" and he looked so much like a girl. Doesn't sound much of a shag to me"! So the thing about him is that he reputedly died of a mixture of alcoholism and syphilis; see, I don't think Flora MacDonald followed him to the shore to wave him ta ta or anything, I think she was going to gob the bastard for drinking her bingo money and giving her vaginal warts.

GAYLE TUESDAY

Hello, I'm, page 3 stunna, Gayle Tuesday. Topless model and rising media star. I ain't joking. Do you like me outfit? Fantastic. I've been doing some promotional work, but I'm not actually at liberty to say which country it is I am pro-moting, obviously. Here's my girl-next-door pout, right. I've got the girl-next-door-but-one, that's completely bent over, but I won't do that now 'cause I've done my back in.

My boyfriend is also my manager, I've got a little nickname for him—I call him pimp.

Here, does anyone remember that Frank MacAvennie, who used to play for West Ham? I've shagged him.

MARK LAMARR

A few years ago I went on holiday to Norfolk for a week. And I went to this town called Wells-next-to-Sea. It's miles from the sea; is that a Norfolk joke, or something? 'Wells-nowhere-near-the-fucking-Sea' it should be called.

And I went there, and it was one of these old communities where people are very proud because they still leave their doors open. Which was great for me because I burgled three houses while I was there.

But I was there in a small town, and sometimes, small towns have small-town attitudes and I didn't have a good time; I remember one night I went into a pub and I walked in, and there was a young girl there, like about a twelve-year-old girl. And she was stood there in this pub with her mum who was the landlady of the pub, and this little girl was just so shocked, she went to her mum, 'Mum, look! Look, Mum, it's Elvis, Mum look, it's Elvis!' And I'm thinking, oh for Christ sake, you know. But I turned round and it was, he lives there.

MARK LAMARR

PAULINE CALF

PAULINE CALF

Listen, I've got something terrible to say. I'm pregnant. Don't ask me who the father is...because I don't know. Only joking. I'll give you a clue; his jackets are designed by Jean Michel Jarre and his shirts, they're by Fettucini, and he wears Kevin Kline underpants. Can you tell? It's Jonathan Ross, yes. Yeah, he's lovely Jonathan, he's got class, like me. Class is like the clap, you've either got it or you haven't; I've got it, and so has Jonathan.

Do you know who I think is absolutely gorgeous? Patrick Swayze. I've seen Dirty Dancing 25 times. The bloke round our way looks just like Patrick Swayze...wears an orthopaedic shoe and works at John Menzies. Oh honest to God he's lovely, really nice. Dead imaginative lover. He'll give me a choice; he'll say things like, 'Pauline, do you want me to make love to you, or do you just want to suck us off?' Do you know what I mean? Variety, it's nice.

But do you know who I can't fucking stand? Sinead O'Connor. Honest to God, she's a right miserable cow, isn't she? I reckon they should get her on the 'Generation Game'. 'Come on Sinead, give us a twirl.' She'd say, 'No, I don't want to.' Hey, Sinead O'Connor—Nothing Compares 2 U—Kojak does, dun't he. I've had him, yeah. I was on top, I said, 'Oh look, I'm on Telly.'

Another one I can't stand—Magenta De Vine. Honest to God. Why does she wear those fucking sunglasses all the time? She looks like Roy Orbison. And the one who really takes the fucking biscuit for me is Carol Vorderman. Honest to God, if she'd been in my class at school, I would have fucking smacked her one. 'Hey, sir, done some sums, aren't I clever?' I've been on countdown with Richard Whitely. Oh, yes, I said come here Richard and show us a bit of your diddle dee dee, doooo [*countdown theme tune*].' He wasn't talking about vowels and consonants in Hatfield Travel Lodge, I tell you that. Oh yes.

JO BRAND

Did you know that there is as much fibre in one bowl of All Bran as there is in nine slices of bread? I'll have the nine slices of bread then, please.

You probably recognise me, because I do a bit of modelling in my spare time. But I haven't quite achieved supermodel status yet. I can't really understand what's the difference between a model and a supermodel, and the only way I can think of to compare it is with regular tampax and super tampax. And there is a similarity, because super tampax are more expensive...and a lot thicker.

And, I just want to talk to you briefly about one of the shittiest films to have come out of America in the last year. *Indecent Proposal*. Did anyone go and see that bollocks, did they? The one where Robert Redford offers Demi Moore a million quid to sleep with him. And the advert over here to make you go and see it was great, because at the end, it said: 'What would you do?'...'Oh, em, er. I don't know??????'...I'd shag him for a fucking tenner, that's what I'd do.

*WHEN VENUS, THE GODDESS OF LOVE, WAS
BORN SHE CHECKED SHE'D GOT EVERY-
THING BEFORE GOING ASHORE.*

parts
of the body

JEFF GREEN

Men's bodies; we have got too much hair on our backsides. I just think women are being so polite not mentioning that. I can't imagine you're getting off on it. Can you imagine a woman looking at her boyfriend when he's stark naked, except for his socks, of course, his blue knee-length ones, trying to look dangerous and it all goes horribly wrong when he drops his contact lens; and he says [*bending over*], 'Bloody hell, where's that gone? Damn! First there's no toilet paper, now I've dropped my fucking contact lens.' I just can't imagine a woman going, 'I love that man, you know. He's so horny.'

PAUL CALF

I know it's not how women are on the outside, 'cause that's not important. It's how they are on the inside, as a human being and their personality. And if they've got big tits that's a bonus.

GAYLE TUESDAY

My boyfriend he's got real respect for me, right, and I think that's important innit? 'Cause the first night we were ever getting off with each other, right, we were snogging and then he started putting his hand up my skirt. So I slapped him and I said, 'Oi you, tits first, I'm not a slag.' You've got to, ain't ya?

But I love my boyfriend, Grant, I love him, he's fantastic. I mean obviously there are the violent mood swings, you know, but nobody's perfect, are they? But he can be ever so moody, right. 'Cause like, the other night we was at this party, right, and we was all laughing 'cause Grant was telling everyone about when one of my boobs got stuck in a window and we was all laughing about it, right. So then I started telling everyone what a tiny penis he had and he got really annoyed about it.

I went to the doctor's the other day. Oh, he was lovely, really nice. Examined my breasts...I only had a verruca. It's funny, though, how men go, 'I'm a tits man, me', 'I'm a bum man, me', 'I'm a legs man, me'. 'Cause girls they never say, 'I'm a bollocks girl, me'.

IAN COGNITO

When I first got into showbusiness, I wanted to be in a rock band and me and the lads in the band we had this brilliant gimmick; what we'd do is we'd get on stage with a couple of rolled up socks down our trousers, and I was the guitarist and I was giving all of that [*thrusts groin forwards*], 'leading with the lunch' we used to call it. And all the girls and the blokes would stand around the front of the stage nudging each other and pointing and giggling. Then we got a manager and he said, 'Look lads, if you're going to get on stage with rolled up socks down your trousers...try shoving them down the front.'

I told my mum that I was going to become a comedian, and she laughed, which I thought was a fucking good start myself. I said, 'Mother, nothing's impossible', and she said, 'Oh, yeah, have you ever tried to shove a turd back up your arse with a spatula?'

ARTHUR SMITH

Why is it, I wonder, that your scrotum looks eighty years older than the rest of your body? Actually, tragically, it doesn't in my case, they look exactly the same.

I often wonder, when it comes to sex, what do men and women want from each other? I was reading in a magazine for heterosexual women the ideal man apparently has the face of Rob Lowe, the body of Daley Thompson and the bottom of Mick Jagger. Well, what a fucking state that bloke would look. Because he would be half black, half white and have an arse that is twenty years older than the rest of his body. Michael Jackson, in fact.

And what is it, what is it that men want from women? I was talking to this bloke the other day, and he said, 'I saw this lovely bird the other day, legs up to her armpits'. Call me wacky, but personally speaking, I prefer a woman with a torso. If the arms go straight into the legs, I just don't know what I'm doing.

JO BRAND

The shittiest film of the year, the one that I thought was really the worst, was that one, *Boxing Helena*. Oh dearie me. I didn't actually go and see it, but if you didn't, it was basically about a woman who got her arms and legs chopped off, and at some point or other was put in a box for some reason. And I was thinking to myself, that if she's in this box and she has a particularly heavy period? Or, a dodgy curry the night before. [*Audience grimaces.*] You're great. You're all going 'Ew' about periods and diarrhoea, I'm actually talking about a woman in a fucking box with both her arms and legs chopped off, but you didn't go 'Ew' about that, did you? You thought, 'Oh, that sounds quite good, we rather like that.'

Let's talk periods, shall we? I think so. You see, a lot of women don't like periods. I love them, I think they're fucking brilliant. Because I have managed to get out of netball at school by having a period . . . for six and a half years. And periods enable me to indulge in my very favourite hobby of lying on my bed, whining quite a lot.

And they can be so useful, can't they, particularly for example if you know someone who lives next door, who you can't stand, who's got a white sofa. Even better if it's from World Of Leather.

But let's face it, the best thing about periods is the fact that people are so embarrassed about them. They go 'Ew, periods are horrible'. And what they do is they use a collection of strange little euphemisms so they don't have to say, 'I've got my period'. And among my favourites are: I've got the painters and decorators in'; 'Arsenal are playing at home'.

But I have to say that my own particular favourite is: 'There's a vast amount of blood squirting out of my cunt, Vicar.'

MAUREEN LIPMAN

'A man goes to a circus owner and says: 'I've got a fantastic act. I call myself The Great Santini. I come on with a fully grown crocodile. I open the crocodile's mouth and I place my private parts in his mouth. The crocodile, of course, closes his mouth, so I pull back my fist, punch him in the eye, his mouth opens in astonishment and I take out my private parts and reveal them unharmed to the audience. They go wild!' The circus owner, amazed by the man's description, offers him a job in the ring. 'You're on tonight', he says, '– and you'd better be good.' That evening the ringmaster announces: 'For the first time in circus history, the one and only daredevil animal act "The Great...Santini"!'

On comes our man, with his giant crocodile. He opens the crocodile's mouth and places his privates in his mouth. The audience gasps as the crocodile closes his mouth. Santini draws back his fist and bops the croc in the eye with all his might and the reptile releases him. Unscathed, Santini shows his undamaged parts to the roaring crowds, says 'Thank you, ladies and gentlemen, thank you. And now you've seen my performance, I wonder is there any brave member of the audience who would like to try to do the same thing?' Silence. Then a tiny old lady in a tam-o'-shanter, in the back row, puts up her hand and calls out: 'Well, I don't mind having a wee go – but can ye not hit me so hard in the eye?'

A man goes to the doctor and announces that he has a complex because his penis is so disgusting. The doctor assures him that most men have a complex about the size and shape of their penis. 'No, but mine's *really* appalling—every woman I've ever shown it to has been horrified.' The doctor reassures him that he's seen just about all kinds of aberrations in his time and he's sure that this one cannot be as bad as he feels it is.

The patient takes off his trousers and shows him. The doctor cannot conceal his astonishment – 'My God!' he gasps, 'that is truly abhorrent. What the . . . ? How the . . . ? I mean, it's like a crumpled . . . I've never seen such a strange . . .'

'Yes, yes——alright,' grumbles the man. 'I know it's a mess, but can you do anything for it?'

'I'm sorry to tell you, but I can't. Not even a plastic surgeon could help you sort that out—you'll just have to live with it.'

A year later the man returns with a minor complaint. The doctor gingerly asks him how is coping with his appalling penis.

'Oh that,' says the fellow. 'That's all fine now. Absolutely cured.'

'Cured?' says the doctor.

'Absolutely,' says the man and he shows him an emasculated penis.

'But how did that happen?' says the doctor, amazed.

'Well, after we spoke I went into the Gents on my way home and I happened to glance into the next cubicle where a man had just finished urinating. I couldn't help noticing that afterwards he merely shook his penis dry.'

'So?' says the doctor. 'What difference does that make to you?'

'Well,' says the man. 'It's simple.' And so saying he grasps hold of his penis and wrings it out like a dishcloth. 'It seems you don't have to do *that* every time after all!'

JEFF GREEN

That was weird that bloke who had a vasectomy under hypnosis, wasn't it? Paul McKenna's going too far as far as I'm concerned.

IAN COGNITO

We're living in a world that puts wings on panty liners. Why? To keep them in place? A quick gust of wind you'll flip over. We don't want wings on panty liners, we want anchors on panty liners, we want grappling hooks on panty liners, we don't want them shifting out of place. 'Cause my girlfriend she bought one of those ones with the unique dry weave that draws everything up into the towel...she's only gone and lost her vag. up there. We were fucking using that as well.

GREG PROOPS

I could be in San Francisco in the sun right now, but I made a choice, I picked London in the spring. Hoo, haa. I'll tell you the reason I came here. I just wanted to come to a country where I'm really good-looking, that's why I came here. Back home it's, 'Hey, Buddy Holly, you some kind of dork?' Here it's, 'Oh, good God, look at him. He's got all his teeth, and his ears are in proportion to his head. What a fox. He's not in the House of Windsor.'

If you go to Texas, USA, and you're a man, they will take you to what is known as a 'titty bar'. It's what passes for culture in Texas. Here they might call it a 'strip joint', a 'live nude show'. In Texas they call it a 'titty bar'. 'You ain't been to a titty bar? You ain't seen shit.' Redneck nirvana. A bunch of guys sitting around in cowboy hats going, 'I got a beer in one hand, I'm looking at tits, I must have fucking died and gone to heaven. If I could shoot a Mexican right now I'd come, I swear to God I would.' And they are fucking everywhere; every single shitty mall has a titty bar in it. You go to some shithole town, and it's like, Toys 'R' Us, Baptist Church, titty bar. Gun shop, titty bar, gun shop, titty bar, gun shop, titty bar, gun shop, titty bar, religious weirdo conflagration place, titty bar.

BEN ELTON

Nobody is prepared for the truth about their bodies, because we see the movies, we see the magazines. In the movies, dicks have twenty-twenty vision, do they not? They always know where they're going; they slip in without a problem, they don't even have to stop snogging, it's just oh, and it's in. No problem at all. Do they use a funnel, is this how it's done? There's none of that probing around for Tom Cruise, is there? There's none of that old 'No, up a bit, down a bit, up, oh, nearly, nearly, no! Not there, wrong fucking hole, get out of there'. No, in it goes.

And once it's in, it stays in. No dick ever comes out mid-shag in the movies, no. No matter how far the bum gets pulled back, the dick is still in. They must be six feet long, they're like telescopes, these dicks. The rest of us, it's like, 'Ah yes, beautiful, beautiful, oh no it's come out...', '...doesn't matter, put it back...', 'I can't fucking find the hole, oh dear...'. Out it comes, and always at the climactic moment. You're just about to come, the best shag you ever had...out it comes, you bash it into your lover's thigh, it bends double, and stabs you in the stomach. You never see that, in the movies. **,**

MAN

Stimulation

The first time my brother saw me in action
he explained that he didn't use his hands at all
and demonstrated how he could achieve excitement
by merely rubbing his knees together.
I copied his method
as I copied many things my brother did
believing him to be a most exemplary boy
but on this occasion my only reward
was a slight abrasion of the knees.

John Hegley

'EMILY, REFINED LADIES DO NOT REVEAL AN ANKLE IN PUBLIC'

BEN ELTON

I know that this is a comedy book but I want to get serious for one moment, ladies and gentlemen. I want to bring up a subject, they asked me not to because it's a bit heavy, it's a bit difficult, and if you don't like it, then fuck off, but I want to talk about it. 'Baywatch'. No, it's a serious subject. 'Baywatch'? Those women on 'Baywatch'? 'Oh they're strong women, positive stereotypes, they save lives, they're strong...'. Not a single pubic hair amongst them! Bald, every single one. Kojak crotches the lot of them. What do they do with all the pubes they must tear out of those poor women on 'Baywatch'? They could stuff a mattress the size of California by now. I mean, it must be like a torture chamber every morning in make-up: 'Next crotch, let's rip them out, there we go, tear them out.' I mean these costumes they wear, you've got room for about one pube behind that, haven't you? I mean, fair enough ladies, if you've got them growing down to your knees, blonde the last six inches, but don't tear them out of your vulva, for God's sake. This is unreal! These smooth little fannies. I mean no chicken skin or pockmarks like most women have, oh no, smooth. They've been sanded down, these fannies. 'Let's buff the next muff!' You could eat your dinner off it. A bit of reality please, these women are life-savers. You'd think there was room on the team for one big old Bertha who didn't give a fuck what was growing out of her crotch, but oh no, there's a man on the set with a magnifying glass going, 'There's a pubic hair on this woman, get her off the set. That's un-American, I want a juvenile fanny there, I want a prepubescent fanny.' What are young women meant to make of this? They're watching it at home, at 5.30 on a Saturday afternoon. They must be thinking that there was something wrong, 'Oh my God, mine are already escaping out of me knickers, and down me leg. Mum, I am the Yeti woman!'

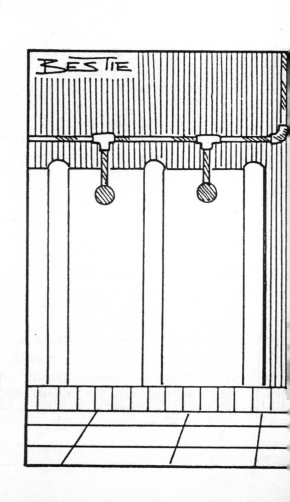

safer
sex

HARRY ENFIELD

AIDS – THE FACTS
A Public Information Bulletin

GREYSON

Good evening. Now, there are a lot of old wives' tales going around about this condition. So let me set the record straight as clearly, concisely and frankly as possible.

Number One. Where does this condition come from? The answer is simple. It was invented by foreigners. Chiefly in the ex-colonies, I'm afraid, such as North America, Kenya, Uganda and of course Tanganyika.

Now we all know how babies are made. A man and a woman get married and on their wedding night they make a bit of a hash of it but after a few days' honeymooning they finally succeed in [*coughs*] and nine months later a baby is born.

This is the British way, at least. And the correct way. Unfortunately, after Independence, the foreigner forgot all we had taught him and started indulging himself in all sorts of depraved acts of [*coughs*], including vile nastiness and beastly unpleasantness.

The result is AIDS, which top scientists have proved is nature's way of giving those people a jolly good wigging.

So, how can we avoid catching this hellish condition? Well, it's perfectly simple.

Never go abroad or talk to foreigners, even on the telephone. If you have to go abroad, in the interests of Trade or Government business, wear pyjamas at all times including under your clothes during the day. Always pull the pyjama cord tight and secure with a knot that only you know how to undo. Shun your friends if their sons have been sent down from school for dormitory activities.

Ensure your parish has a vicar who's married.

Carry your own lavatory seat with you at all times.

Identify these. [*Holds up condom.*] These are called prophylactics. Keep a sharp eye out for anyone purchasing them from the chemist, for he or she is a pervert. Protect your neighbourhood from these people. Spread rumours. You might like to set your dogs on them and hound them out of their homes.

So let me set your mind at rest on various matters about which you may have been fretting.

You cannot catch AIDS from having an early evening pick-me-up with your wife, be it a gin and tonic or a whisky and soda.

Nor can you catch it from having a bath—but avoid public swimming pools.

And most importantly, you can't catch it from having bedtime [*coughs*] in the correct British manner, which we all know is a fearful business, but nevertheless one in which we must indulge if we are to produce sons for the nation.

God Bless the Queen.

Harry Enfield

JO BRAND

‘One time that I did lie down for about four days was when I was trying to get a femidom in. And it was a bit sad, because there wasn't even a bloke around. I was just practising really. Femidoms are a fucking nightmare. Who invented them? Was it a bloke? I think it probably was. Because if you look at it, condoms were the one contraceptive left that men had to manage on their own... 'Oh no, we can't manage that, could you make some for the girls, please?'

And so they did. Not so much female condoms, more like Tesco's carrier bags, from what I can make out. What a fucking nightmare if one of those falls out of your handbag in the pub. 'Oh, it's alright, I'm just off on a ballooning weekend.' And ecologically, a bad idea. Epping Forest is going to look like a jellyfish graveyard. It's going to be horrid.

And I've read all these articles about it, and no one really tells you how to put one in when you're reading about it. I assumed you had to use one of those big long wooden poles that teacher used to shut the top window with at primary school—with the old hook on the end for safety.

Yes. I really am going to try them properly, though, but I'm not going to tell the next bloke I sleep with that they're for a woman. No. New standard male European size, that's what I'm going to say. 'Oh dear, bit of a tiny one down there, darling?'

JEREMY HARDY

‘I was a bit perturbed by the front page of the *Sunday Mirror* this morning about sweetie-flavoured condoms for the under-16s, because when I was under 16, sex with a condom was sex *with* a condom; nobody else was involved, it was a very intimate, private, protestant experience.

MORWENA BANKS

MORWENA BANKS

'Yes, I do know what is the AIDS. It is when two men and a lady do go into a smelly toilet and stick knitting needles up their hairy bum bums and blood does spurt out what is made up of poisonous jelly, and they do put it in a cup and do drink it, and they say: yum yum, this is very tasty. But it is not really because there are little monsters in it which go climb up inside your gully, and make you all purple wif spots on, and you do turn into, un yeah, you turn into a scary umpire. And if someone wot haves got the AIDS does lick you or sit next to you on the bus, you will shrivel up into a hairy monkey, and then you can only say: 'Cooeee, mister shifter?' And next you will turn into a skellington that must poo in a special bag and be sick on a plate. And if you do die of it you get frown into a pit with snakes and everyone will pretend that you did die of a bump on the head. And Baby Jesus will be furious and say 'Get out of heaven, it is your own fault for biting bare bottoms. Thank you, goodbye.' And you can catch the AIDS from eating cake wif spit on it, or from drinking wee, or touching a black baby, or from kissing Princess Diana. And that is what is the AIDS, it is, it's *true*!'

LYNN FERGUSON

'Did you know that the first condoms were actually made out of silk and tied on with a little ribbon? Didn't stop you getting pregnant or anything, but they were a fuck of a lot easier to deal with when you were pissed, no? Now, my ex-boyfriend used to get steaming so often I had one surgically attached, you know, to help him find the lower half of his body really, and that didn't help, so I had a little bell attached to the end of it. It wasn't for any more sexual gratification or anything, but the cat enjoyed it.'

JEFF GREEN

'If men don't like wearing contraceptives, get ribbed condoms, they're the best. 'Cause you can wear them inside out, can't you fellers, it's a very good idea. Your girlfriend's going, 'I can't feel a thing.' And you're gong, 'I can—these are brilliant.' She says, 'You bastard, it's inside out.' 'Piss off. I bought them. It's my pound in the slot. Your pound your side, my pound my side.'

French letters, English words

A poem about condoms was requested
I'll see what I can come up with I jested
and I considered the phrase 'electronically tested'
and imagined the poor little things
shot through with voltage and pain
and thought of starting a campaign
to stop it
and I thought about the campaign
to tell penis-users they might cop it
without one, a condom not a penis, that is,
Protection and collection
in those little rubber teats
is something that can save your life
and also save your sheets.

▶ 83   **John Hegley**

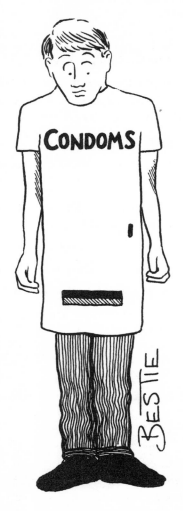

THE CATALOGUE HAD PROMISED THAT THE SPECIALLY DESIGNED T-SHIRT WOULD MAKE HIM LOOK LIKE A SEX MACHINE

A Sketch. Liberal Fascist couple, **PETER** and **JENNIFER WELLS**, are sitting at a desk sifting through leaflets. There is a telephone to hand.

Peter: What's all this bumph, Jennifer?

Jennifer: I've signed us up as friends of The Terrence Higgins Trust. This is all their safe sex literature...[*she hands pamphlets to Peter*]...I think we should become Buddies.

Peter: Oh, we get on alright, don't we?

Jennifer: No, no, a Buddy. It's where we look after someone with HIV.

Peter: Now, wait a moment. I'm willing to become a nodding acquaintance, but that's it.

Jennifer: Oh, don't be so mean, Peter. After all, we might get a famous one.

Peter: All the famous ones are dead, aren't they?

Jennifer: Oh yes. Never mind, I'm sure there'll be some more coming along soon.

Peter: But I don't want to schlepp up to the hospital every week.

Jennifer: Oh no Peter, I think our Buddy comes and stays with us.

[*Pause. Peter digests information.*]

Peter: Now wait a minute, Jennifer, I am on the verge of a rather tasty promotion. If you think I'm about to start living with the cast of *La Cage aux Folles*, you've got another think coming.

Jennifer: Peter, it's only one of them.

Peter: Yes, but you know what that mob are like. They can't go for a pint without picking somebody up—I don't want to end up with the Village People rimming each other on the new Persian throw-rug.

Jennifer: Oh yes; well look, Peter, we can have strict house rules: one visitor a day, under supervision, lights out 7 o'clock.

Peter: And he doesn't touch the cutlery.

Jennifer: And he doesn't touch the cutlery.

Peter: To be honest, Jennifer, when you suggested joining this Higgins Trust club, I did imagine that our involvement would be slightly less...

Jennifer: ...involved

Peter: Exactly. I thought we'd slip them a tenner every month and no questions asked. At the very most we'd get a nice Mapplethorpe print.

Jennifer: Yes, that lovely one of the broomstick.

Peter: No, I don't think it's a broomstick, Jennifer. Basically, I just didn't expect to have to sleep with the buggers.

Jennifer: Peter! Don't be so homophobic. This disease doesn't just effect the poof community, you know.

Peter: Oh that's right. It's really cut a swathe through the golf club. I wondered why it was so easy to get a round recently. I thought it was something to do with the recession, but oh no, silly me, a killer virus is targeting people who wear checked trousers and diamond pattern V-necks.

Jennifer: Now, in addition, you've got to wear this red ribbon.

[*Jennifer hands him ribbon.*]

Peter: Jennifer, I might as well just go out wearing a big badge saying 'arse for hire'.

Jennifer: Peter, it's not all arses, you know.

Peter: [*Holding up pamphlet*] Really, well look, safer sex for gay men, and I quote 'Licking arse is safe', 'You could play with his arse', 'You can stick your fingers up his arse, put dildos or butt plugs', guess where?—'up his arse'. It does seem a little arse-heavy, don't you think, Jennifer?

Jennifer: Mmmmm. Do you think you put the plug in first or last? Is it to keep things falling out or to stop things going in?

Peter: Oh, I don't think you put everything in at the same time. I imagine it's an either/or situation.

Jennifer: Oh I see, fingers or dildo.

Peter: Fist or basketball.

Jennifer: Butt plug or hamster.

Peter: Exactly. Listen to this, Jennifer. 'You can play with cock rings or nipple clamps or try playing with piss, oil, mud or beer.' I mean, is this sex or the First World War? My taxes are paying for this piss fest, are they? No, I'm sorry, but I really can't sponsor this.

Jennifer: I must say though, Peter, this position is a bit rich coming from you. What about that time at boarding school?

Peter: It's not true! It didn't happen. It was 20 years ago. It didn't happen and it didn't happen 20 years ago.

Jennifer: Alright, alright.

Peter: We all had girlfriends in my dorm, oh yes.

Jennifer: If you say so.

Peter: Yes, the tuck shop didn't even sell chocolate digestives, so there's absolutely no question of us standing around in a circle...

Jennifer: ...and playing spunky biscuit.

Peter: Exactly. Never heard of the game. Just get on the phone, I'm cancelling our subscription.

[*Jennifer dials*]

Jennifer: Hello, Jennifer Wells here. There's been a terrible mistake. My husband and I thought we were signing up for the Reader's Digest...

Peter: Give it here.

[*Peter takes the phone. He is now wearing plastic gloves.*]

Peter: Hello, Peter Wells here. Could you put me straight through to Mr Higgins-Trust, please? Oh sorry, I'd assumed it was a double-barrelled name. So who am I talking to? Quentin. Well there you are, I think we've isolated your first problem. Now far be it from me to tell you how to run your business, but staffing it exclusively with a bunch of soft lads called Quentin is not the sort of thing to endear you to normal people. That's my first point.

Secondly, would it be possible to divert some of your money to the RSPCA? Something that people actually care about. That tin I could take round the golf club, you know? Get the whole thing a bit more legitimate, above board. Basically lessen the whole poof angle. Oh I'm sorry, it's not 'poof' any

PETER AND
JENNIFER WELLS

longer. Will 'gay' do? Oh it's 'queer' now, is it? Well, while you're on, perhaps you could put me straight on a few others?

[*Takes out pen. Gives it to Jennifer.*]

Peter: How about, 'Friend of Dorothy's'? No. 'Big Girl's Blouse'? 'Flower Arrangers...'?

Jennifer: Ask him about 'sly butcher'.

Peter: What about 'sly butcher'? Yes we've never been too sure ourselves. We've always imagined it's something to do with taking your meat round the back. Yes.

Jennifer: Ask him about 'coloured'.

Peter: Yes look, while we're about it, can you help us with this whole 'black/coloured' question? You can? Oh you're black? Jesus Christ, that's a bit of a double whammy, isn't it?

Jennifer: Ask if he can get Justin Fashanu's autograph.

Peter: Can you get us Justin Fashanu's...Hello? The bugger's hung up.

Jennifer: [*indicating bumph*] So what are we going to do with all this lot.

Peter: Let's just bin it, shall we?

Jennifer: Oh no, we should recycle it, send it back to the Higgins Trust.

Peter: Yes, they can scrumple it all up and make it into butt plugs.

love
and emotion

MAID MARIAN SUSPECTED ROBIN WASN'T QUITE
READY FOR AN EMOTIONAL INVOLVEMENT

PAUL CALF

I'm still missing my girlfriend, Julie. She's pissed off. I've written her this letter to try and get her back; see if you think this will do the trick:

Dear Julie

I can't stop thinking about you. We had some good times and some bad times. Remember when I was sick in the back of that taxi and he threw us out in the middle of the Peak District at 2 o'clock in the morning in the pouring rain and all we had was half a can of lager? And then there were the bad times as well; like when we didn't have any lager at all.

Yesterday I found your boob tube in the boot of my Cortina. I remember the last time you wore it; it was that night I was set upon by five students and I fucking leathered the lot of them. Why can't it always be like that? I'll never forget that look on your face, that night shagging in the back of my car. I wish it had been me. I want you to know I will change. I'm trying to give up two of my worst habits, smoking and masturbation, which I'm finding difficult as I'm a twenty-a-day man and I smoke like a chimney.

Love

Paul (Calf)

PAULINE CALF

6 I'm trying to write this novel for Mills and Boon. I've written this first draft. It's called *Stallion Heart* by Paulette Vache. (That's my pen name—Vache. That's French for cow. Don't know what calf is, probably petite vache or something like that...)

Stallion Heart

Her name was Polly Lamb, she was small and petite, a size eight, but with a full bosom where weary travellers would oft rest their weary heads. She was the barmaid of the Old Traveller's Lodge up near Hatfield.

One day a tall dark stranger rode into the courtyard and alighted from a black stallion. He seemed to dance across the cobbles. It was a daring dance, a delicious dance, a dirty dance.

She took his coat and looked inside at the label, it said Lord Patrick of Swayze. It was made of real cashmere and was from Next for Men. Without further ado, she took him to her bedchamber, reached inside his roughshod breeches, and there discovered his stallion-like manhood.

Within forty minutes and five he had shot his load thricefold. At last, thought Pauline, I've met a man who's dead sophisticated. I will endeavour to get to know him.

GREG PROOPS

'So I want to say happy birthday to my wife tonight, it is my wife's birthday. And I'll tell you, I've known her for ten years, we've been married for five years and she's...ah you guys...she's fifteen now, and...just kidding!...She's twelve...she's one of Jerry Lee Lewis's cousins.

And I don't know if this happens to you at your house, but this happened to me the other night. I'm watching the game on TV, and my wife is yelling at me from the other end of the house through the whole fucking game. So, I'm trying to watch the game, and she's like, 'Greg, come here.'
I'm like, 'What?'
'Greg, come here, it's really important, Greg.'
'What is it, Jennifer?'
'Greg, you've got to come here. It's really important.'
So I go all the way to the other end of the house...
'Greg—look at what the cat's doing.'
'No Jennifer, you look at what the cat's doing.' [*Kicks cat*]
So we came up with a little compromise in my abode, which is from now on, during the game, she is only allowed to say one phrase. Now, before you think I'm some sort of big macho dickhead, huge-pizza-sized-nipple-arsehole guy, I want you to know that I had to make some compromises too. For instance, during sex now, I have to say, or squeal like a pig, rather... 'My pain is your pleasure, Mighty Mistress of Darkness.' Not something I'm overly proud of, but as I say, marriage is based on compromise. So from now on she's only allowed to say one phrase during the game. And that phrase is: 'Here is your sandwich, my well-hung warlord.'

JEFF GREEN

We should have been told how to sleep with someone. I don't mean sex, I mean when you sleep with a girl and it's your first girlfriend and it's a beautiful thing, but you can't get any kip.

Your first chance is normally on a single bed and you don't stand a chance. It's, 'Hello, crikey, we're not two pieces of Lego, are we? Do you think we should sleep top and tail?' 'No, if you love me it's face to face.' 'I do love you, but we don't fit together.'

DINOSAURS DIED OUT DURING THE PLATONIC PERIOD

Men should have holes here [*points to his breast area*]. One person should have a nose, the other shouldn't. And when you're breathing in, they're breathing out. You think, 'That's pure carbon dioxide I'm breathing here. She's trying to kill me.' What do you do with your arm? There's always an arm left...Yours, basically.

'Are you comfortable?'

'**N**o I'm fucking not comfortable. Do you seriously think if I was on my own, I'd go, "Here's for a good night's sleep. I'll get my arm and wrap it right round the back of my head, so that all the tendons rip"?'

And that twitch, you know that twitch you never even knew you had. You've never twitched in your life, then someone lies beside you and just as you're nodding off, you get a little embarrassing spasm.

'**W**hat the fuck was that?'

'**D**on't know, do I? I never twitched until you showed up.'

I always try and disguise it.

'**U**m, er, just off to the toilet, I think.'

MARK LAMARR

We've got an incredible show for you. I can honestly say, the finest acts currently performing comedy in the whole of Britain have influenced the people you'll be seeing tonight, and what we've tried to do is to make it a show you'll remember, like the best show that you've ever been to in your whole life. So when you see other people who are here, you'll go up to them and say, 'Hey, do you remember "Filth"? What a great night, it was the best night of my whole life.' But sadly, I look out and I see a sea of faces who might see people who are here tonight and when you see them you'll go, 'Alright?'

Some people, that's what they do, it's the sum total of their emotion. You've just won a million pounds, 'Oh, alright.' You see them a lot on 'The Generation Game'. Bruce says, 'Right, you've got 20 million people watching and you've got a funny story, haven't you?'

And they go, 'I fucking haven't, what are you on about?'

And he says, 'Go on. Tell your funny story about when you met.'

And they're going, 'What are you fucking doing to me, Bruce?'

There are just some people who don't show any emotion.

I've been reading this book about a bloke called David Livingstone, quite a famous explorer. I read in this book that apparently, you know how nowadays rich blokes shag models and take drugs (and I'm just saying that because I've got a few quid), but in the last century, they used to go exploring. And David Livingstone, what he wanted to do was find the source of the Nile, 4,000 miles of river and go, 'There it is,' and then fuck off home. That was his little thing in life that he wanted to do.

So he went to the Nile—and he got lost, which I can't work out. How do you get lost when you're following a river? I'm not an expert on these things, but surely, there's a wet bit, that's the river, and you stay quite close to that on the dry bit until you get to the end. But he got completely lost and he was lost there for two years in 'darkest' Africa. That's what he called it when he got back because no one had ever been there before. But I've seen it on TV...That's quite a bright place, Africa. That's a really poor excuse for getting lost: 'It was fucking dark, I couldn't find the river.'

But while he was there, he discovered the Zambezi. He found that. Seventeen hundred miles of water, *he* found the Zambezi...which was a big shock to the Africans living there at the time, they couldn't fucking believe it. They went, 'He's a sharp fucker, that David Livingstone. He's only been here five minutes, he just discovered that. I was swimming in that last week, I can't believe it. Thousands of generations of my family have bathed in that river—he found it. What a sharp bloke.'

But anyway, he was lost there for two years, in 'darkest' Africa as he called it, and the British Government sent out a bloke called Henry Stanley to go and find him. And it took him two years but eventually he found him, and there was the famous exchange, when he went up to him, put his hand out, and said, 'Doctor Livingstone, I presume?'...which I thought was a bit sarky to be honest. You're rubbing it in now, because if he's the only white man ever to have been there, it's him isn't it? Unless you're a really stupid bloke and you just ask everyone you meet; he could be on the buffet at Brighton or something, and he's going, 'Doctor Livingstone, I presume?', and they're going, 'Nah, he's in Africa, isn't he?'

But I just try to imagine what it must have been like for David Livingstone. He'd been out there for two years, and was probably thinking, 'I can't find the end of the river. I'm never going to get back to Scotland, see all the people I love and everything...' And it must have been such a moving experience. But apparently what happened was that Henry Stanley went up to him and said, 'Doctor Livingstone, I presume?' and Doctor Livingstone went... 'Alright?'

A beautiful thing happened recently. I was walking home from the pub at about closing time, and there was a young bloke outside the pub. And he was with a young girl who was about fifteen, leaning against the wall, and I assume he was her boyfriend. And he was sort of leaning over her and chatting her up, and she was sort of being chatted up and he said one of the most beautiful things I've ever heard. He said to her, 'I don't want to make love to you...I want to go and get a kebab,' and it just, you know, touched my heart.

GREG PROOPS

Riding around on the train in London is like the furtive glance capital of the world. No one will look you in the eye. Everyone's riding around, reading their *Evening Standard*; maybe they accidentally look up and make eye-contact; they're like, 'AARRGHH!' Because if a Londoner looked another human in the eye, then they'd experience an emotion, and that would be very wrong, wouldn't it, ladies and gentlemen? It would be against London law.

HELL IS OTHER PEOPLE
A Short Story by Sean Hughes

'Another painless day of work over' he catch-phrased to his chums as they stood in the crowded space of The George, a pub deemed OK for a quick one, before home offered a more comfortable seating arrangement. In fact, the pub had changed beyond reason over the last year: techno music blasted out, trendy haircuts scared away the tourists and the beer was warm. They talked about the day's events in their insular world. Ken was always destined to work in television; the name was made to roll off the credits of every bland variety show ever made. To the outsider, working in TV must seem so exciting. Little do they realise it's just an office job, a bunch of people gathered together to make a product. All pettiness, no passion. Somewhat like politicians who enter their field for all the right reasons, only to be dragged down by the 'don't rock the boat' police. The lesson is never learnt—the trimmings are the trappings. Ken was depressing himself; another drink was called for. On the surface he had all the attributes needed to be profiled in a fashion magazine: TV producer, a lovely wife, huge house, many trips abroad, member of several select clubs and a pretty good drug dealer.

And here he was with similar types deep in their shallow conversation, a group of men with a collected swagger to match. Drink was drunk. Four males plus alcohol results in the IQ being divided by twenty. They were at the patting each other's back stage; one more drink and they would hover above the ground, fancying themselves beyond reach. They deserved each other. Ken caught the eye of a beautiful woman, well, more accurately, the lips. This woman had sensational lips, pouting, kissing her own dyed blonde hair. She was of the Wonder Bra generation. She knew how to highlight her good points. Ken was cynical of this yet couldn't help fancying her; he imagined mad, fumbling sex with her. He saw her approach what he decided was her boyfriend. It annoyed him so to see beautiful women with guys he deemed below himself. Ken had lost interest in whatever conversation he had been in. Talking shop bored him, most things bored him. Ken was now at a peep show hunting out any number of feminine shapes, the open-cut dresses, the tight leather trousers, the fuck-me eyes. He thought he'd married too young, hadn't played the field enough, but never had any intention of being unfaithful. Susan offered much more than sex, but sometimes that was all he craved. He hadn't enjoyed sex with Susan for a long while. It was nearly dilemma time—she was having maternal instincts and they were both at the age where most of their friends were having abortions—and yet they never discussed any of this. Such private, important talks were kept for those beery evenings with the boys.

The bell called, goodbyes were slurred. The taxi journey a horny blur, Ken got in the door, dropped his briefcase, huffed into the chair, flicked on the telly, realised quickly there was nothing on worth watching, missed the irony, washed his face, brushed his teeth, flossed his teeth, gargled between his teeth, admired his teeth, fell into bed. Susan was asleep. He was aroused; he hugged her, she didn't budge, he shifted around pretending to get comfortable, he kissed her back, felt her thigh. Soon they were facing each other, both excited. Ken kissed her lips, pretending they were the ones from earlier on, he fondled her breasts imagining he'd just taken off the Wonder Bra, he closed his eyes and was now making love to the nameless person. It felt good, and it got better as he took turns fucking the various shapes he had encountered earlier on. He still wasn't erect. His mind went into overdrive. In the middle of his mad frenzy Susan appeared: he was imagining sleeping with the person he was actually sleeping with. This terrified him. He adored Susan and didn't want to drag her down with him. He tried to stop himself but his eyes refused to open and he was about to orgasm. It was torture as Susan, unaware of his hell, willed him on. Ken came in his darkness. He died a little. A mandatory hug later he rolled over onto his side and felt very alone, very troubled, very frustrated, very evil. What had he become? What had he let himself turn into? Was he capable of love any more, had he ever been capable; had he just pretended that love was involved? Something had to be done, drastic action was called for. He was sick of just letting things happen; it was time for a change. 'I want a divorce,' Susan said.

politics

ARTHUR SMITH

To me it's a great tragedy when you start to think about sex. I look around, I don't know, about 80 per cent of the people reading this have never had sex under a Labour administration. I speak as a man who has done it under the Liberals. Gertrude Stein, she was a cracker.

JO BRAND

A bit of bad news for women lately. Apparently, some judge said there was no such thing as PMT. Fuck, no more shoplifting for us then, girls.

IAN COGNITO

This country, it makes illegal all the fucking wrong things. I found out today in the *Observer*, apparently the Tories are corrupt; now there's a big fucking surprise for you. 'Cause there's an old saying, 'How do you know when a Tory's lying? Answer—'Cause you can see their lips move.' So what do they do?—they give us a Prime Minister with no fucking top lip. They're all at it.

Sixteen-year-old people can't have sex with sixteen-year-old people, no matter what their proclivity is, and Teddy Taylor, the MP for fucking Southend, he said, 'We do not want-sixteen-year-old kids being sucked into a gay lifestyle.' Fucking brilliant—I don't even have to bother writing them sometimes.

This world, this world's gone mad, it's fucking left me behind. We're living in the sort of country that prints Ambulance the wrong way round on the front of an ambulance...just in case some fucker's driving along, looks in the mirror and goes, 'Here, there's an ecnalubma behind us. What the fuck's one of them, then?' We live in a world that's invented the Ketchip, a chip with ketchup in the middle for those kids that are too fucking stupid to put it on for themselves. People are starving in the world and someone's invented a machine that puts ketchup in a chip. Well done, just what we fucking needed.

JEREMY HARDY

'But, eh, your man Patten wants to clamp right down on your sex education. Can you imagine John Patten-style sex education? Such moralistic education would be terrible. You'd have 10-year-olds being taught biology and the teacher would say, 'So, 1C, pay attention, we're going to talk about human reproduction. Here we see the human organs in cross-section; here we see the man penis...or devil's water pistol, to give it its scientific name; and here is the very pit of the loins, the sperms...Satan's tadpoles. See how they writhe, ready to fertilise the eggs, which jiggle and disport themselves provocatively in the lewd, foul, dank cave of the harlot's lust? Any questions at all?' And that poor headmistress, Jane Brown, got all the stick for saying a stupid thing about *Romeo and Juliet* in Hackney. But headmistresses are supposed to tell children that God loves them and that she can hear them in the staff room when it's at the other end of the fucking school. So she refused tickets for *Romeo and Juliet* because she said it was too heterosexual, when she should have said that it was about underage sex and the right wing would have been on her side. Tory MPs saying, 'Well, thank God somebody has spoken out at last against this politically correct Shakespeare – who is he anyway?' And the tabloids would have praised Jane, saying, 'PLUCKY HEAD SAYS NO TO ITIE CHILD-PORN-DANCE Shove it, Shaky, go back to Brum, says crusading Jane.'

They're very worried, the Tories, because they want to protect the young, which is why they wouldn't reduce the age of consent for homosexual men from 21 to 16; they kept it at 18 because they think that young men need to be protected from buggery...or at the very least paid for it. And it conjures up images of older men preying on the young; 16- and 17-year-olds in sixth form colleges, and outside these seedy old men in raincoats going, 'Here son, give us a blow job'. 'Oh, right-ho, guvnor.' And they're worried about gay teachers because they think the teachers will pass it on. How? How will the teacher pass it on? You don't emulate your teacher's lifestyle; if you did we'd all be walking around in corduroy jackets with elbow patches.

GAYLE TUESDAY

‘But along with all my topless work, obviously I try to do as
much charity work as possible. I did a sponsored walk,
Topless for the Mentally Handicapped. And I do have a
couple of campaigns. One of the things I don't believe
in, I don't believe in testing make-up on animals, right. I
think that's disgusting. Because apparently, they've got
these rabbits now wearing lipstick. I mean, for goodness
sake...a rabbit's main worry is its facial hair problem. And I
think this whole testing make-up on animals is very dangerous. 'Cause I knew this one bloke who was going out with a
woman, a very heavily made up woman, for six weeks before
he found out she was a rabbit.

Now don't get me wrong, I don't hate feminists, no I don't...I
feel sorry for them. 'Cause it's ever so sad, right. I read in the
Sunday Sport, their feet are webbed—that's why they can't
wear high heels. Well, it's awful, innit? I'm not having a go,
but the thing about these feminist-types is they don't understand the law of nature. 'Cause men, you see, men by nature
they're hunters, hunter-gatherers. A man goes out, don't he?
A man goes out, out the back; he's providing the food for his
woman, the shelter, he's collecting all the sticks, he's often
very busy, he comes back, he sews the seed amidst the womb
of woman and then mankind proceeds throughout and therefore and thereonwards and therefore and thereon there...

Now, I did explain this funnily enough to Germaine Greer.
Straight over her head. And that is what we're up against with
these feminist-types...ignorance. And the thing about
Germaine, I think underneath it all she'd rather be
blonde with big tits and going out with a big star
like Jim Davidson. She won't admit it, will she?**’**

Steve Bell

BLAST! BASICS BULLETIN BOARD: IF MEMBERS ARE IN ANY DOUBT AT ALL ABOUT ANY ASPECT OF THEIR BEHAVIOUR THEY MUST CONSULT THE WHIPS OFFICE

TELL ME: IS IT ALL RIGHT TO MASTURBATE?

I'LL GET BACK TO YOU

NORMAN — I'M BEING SWAMPED WITH ENQUIRIES — WHERE EXACTLY DOES THE PARTY STAND ON MASTURBATION?

I THINK THE POSITION IS WE DON'T STAND TO MASTURBATE, BUT I'LL HAVE TO CHECK....

LISTEN — I'VE SPOKEN TO NORMAN, AND HE SAYS MASTURBATION MAY BE PERMISSIBLE AS LONG AS YOU'RE LYING DOWN....

...BUT HE'S NOT PRONOUNCING DEFINITELY UNTIL HE'S SPOKEN TO REPRESENTATIVES FROM THE CHURCH AND THE POLICE FORCE

LAMBETH PALACE? I NEED TO SPEAK TO THE FLYING BISHOP URGENTLY!!

FLYING BISHOP SPEAKING: HOW CAN I BE OF ASSISTANCE?

BISHOP — I NEED TO KNOW: IS MASTURBATION WRONG? HOW FIRMLY SHOULD WE CONDEMN IT?

IT'S A TICKLISH ISSUE. THERE ARE DEFINITE DRAWBACKS TO THE SIN OF ONAN. HOW TO HANDLE IT — THERE'S THE RUB...... WE'LL BE WITH YOU IN A COUPLE OF SHAKES!!

D.F.E. TO FLYING BISHOPS; D.F.E. TO FLYING BISHOPS!

D.F.E. THIS IS FLYING BISHOPS; WHAT'S YOUR PROBLEM?

FLYING BISHOPS: THIS IS D.F.E: I WANT YOU TO COME DOWN HARD ON SEX IN SCHOOLS!

D.F.E.: THIS IS FLYING BISHOPS: — YOU SAUCY CREATURE!!

© Steve Bell 1994

IAN COGNITO

I want you to know that I can deal with hecklers, 'cause you're all scared to heckle, and I don't blame you, 'cause I'm fucking brilliant with hecklers, alright. Watch. [*To people in front row of audience.*] You're ugly, you're stupid, Ha—you're a girl, and let's face it, you two, I don't think we'll be seeing you in the next episode of 'Baywatch', will we now? I will just say only one person's ever got the better of me, but a couple of weeks after he did, he ended up with a plastic bag over his head, a flex round his neck and a fucking orange in his mouth. Bear it in mind.

LYNN FERGUSON

I love all that Stephen Milligan stuff. Thank you, comedy gods. There was a beautiful thing happened in Scotland with it, 'cause there was a lot of panic up there 'cause there was only three Tory MPs or something; and this guy in the West Coast of Scotland held a constituency meeting and everybody was shitting themselves, going 'What's he going to say? Is it the end of the Tory party?' And he got them in the meeting and announced, 'I'd just like to say that if I'm ever found dead with a bag over my head it is definitely murder.'

JO BRAND

And some laws have come out recently that have upset me quite a lot—the anti-squatting laws—because I just don't think I can piss standing up.

MARK THOMAS

Those Tories who were discussing the age of consent for gay men, I don't know if you saw them on the telly, fucking mad, absolutely rabid. 'No you can't have it happen, naughty, bible says no tiny things, throbby vessels, spurt, spurt, mustn't happen, no, no, unnatural.' And you're thinking, *unnatural?* I'm looking at fucking inbreeding that Crufts would envy, and you say 'unnatural'? These people's chromosomes must look like a bad hand at fucking Scrabble!

MARK LAMARR

Tell me if this is fair or not. I got done for speeding recently, and I had to go to court. And I was speeding, so fair enough. But the case was: The Queen versus Mr Lamarr. Whose word are they going to take there, you know? Luckily, she never turned up. I went to court as a kid, for shoplifting. And they say, if you show remorse and you admit to other offences, that goes in your favour. So I went in – I went to a magistrate's court, and I thought, 'show remorse, admit to other offences.' And he said, 'Do you always drive this fast, Mr Lamarr?', so I went, 'Oh, fuck me, yeah – cor blimey, every time I get in a car, a ton at least, you know.'

PAUL CALF

I'm not sexist. Women say, 'Paul, you're sexist.' I'm not, I'm a radical feminist. I think you've gotta be these days if you wanna get your end away.

GREG PROOPS

I am The Proclaimers. And I would drive five hundred miles, and I would drive five hundred more, to be the bespectacled, four-eyed, myopic piece of shit to fall down and make a penis

GREG PROOPS

reference at your door. You might have seen my skinny Buddy Holly, biscuit-headed ass on 'Whose Line Is It Anyway?'. They show it in the United States now. And I think the difference between here and there is: someone here might come up to me and go, 'Oh, I've seen you on "Who's Line Is It Anyway?"' and I'm like, 'Really?' and they say, 'Yeah, you're shit.'– England, ha. In the States people come up and they go, 'Hey, man...how does that scoring work?' and I'm like, 'It's a joke.' 'Fuck, I'll say it's a joke! You were the best one and you lost by like a billion points, dude. What is wrong with that bald fucker?' Because in the festive land where I come from, there is a marked lack of irony... Ronald Reagan for eight years, George Bush for four years, I rest my case.

sexuality

PAUL CALF

Do you know what? I think it's great, this, I think it's really good, this book for The Terrence Higgins Trust. 'Cause I'm not prejudiced, you know. I don't care who you are; you can be gay, straight, bisexual, homosexual, black, white. I don't care who you are; if you give me grief you get the shit kicked out of you, alright.

LILY SAVAGE

My mother, when she wants to talk about something that she doesn't understand, she mutters. So you say to her, 'How's your mate?', she'll go, 'She's not well.' 'So what's up with her?' [*muttered*] 'She's got cancer.' Or she'll say, 'Do you know those two women up the road who live together?' and I say 'Yeah', and she says, 'They're uh uh.' I said, 'They're what?' 'Uh uh.' I was twenty-four before I discovered a gay woman wasn't called a 'uh uh'. And me mother would go on a coach trip, and I'd say 'What was York like?' And she'd say, 'Oh, the toilets were beautiful.' Or if she went into a restaurant, I'd say, ' What was it like?' and she'd say, 'Oooo, you should have seen the toilets!' All those years my mother was a cottage queen and I never knew. Fucking hell, just shows you.

RHONA CAMERON

I don't like going abroad, because every year we make this mistake, well I do, that you go through the stock process of 'I need a holiday, I need to relax, I need to unwind, I need to go away and pay hundreds of pounds to have people fucking stare at me all day.' Because you're on your first day in a different place and people do stare at you, don't they? They stare and stare. You'd think some of those families had never seen two drunken lesbians fist-fucking on a beach before.

Ooops. I wasn't going to say that. I'm not a lesbian all the time, just sometimes when it suits me. Because I'm not going out with anyone anyway, because my girlfriend actually left me and went back to her old boyfriend...because he's got a bigger penis than I do. And he doesn't have to carry his around in a plastic bag either. (That's me banned from the sisterhood meetings now.)

GREG PROOPS

I come from San Francisco, which is the gay capital of the United States. It's not official, it's just a little thing. So wherever you go in the United States, people are very sensitive. 'Hey man, where you from?' 'San Francisco.' 'Oh. [*Snigger*] You must be some kind of fagelope?' Yeah, as if gay people are coming to your house in the middle of the night, knocking on your door, going, 'Get up. Get up. You're straight now, but you're going to be gay by morning. I mean it, Mister. This isn't an outing, this is an in-ing. We're doing the whole family. First, we're going to redo the living room. This place is a fucking mess, girlfriend, get a grip.'

JEREMY HARDY

'In America Clinton's trying to let gay men into the Army and the Army says, 'No, we can't have gays in the Army, 'cause it's a male preserve, it's about morale, all men together and having showers naked and they have to go off in the forest and stay in tents for months, all together, all men, and then run around in the forest stripped to their waist in combat trousers...'

Which means it's a bit pointless joining the army if you're not gay; there's fuck all in it for anyone else. It's just the Village People writ large. And a lot of men don't like lesbians, because, they say, if a woman is a lesbian she won't want to do it with them...completely ignoring the fact that even were she not a lesbian, there is still every chance that she wouldn't want to go to bed with them.

And people say it's unnatural to be gay, but the people who say that are always dressed from head to toe in polyester. What does nature matter? Babies' incubators aren't natural, dialysis machines aren't natural, body scanners aren't natural; I'll tell you what's natural: natural is earthquakes, wasps, stinging nettles, shit, piss, pain and Quorn.

And religious bigots point to Leviticus. They say Leviticus tells us homosexuality is a sin: Chapter 18 verse 22 says it's an abomination. Well, it does, but Leviticus says all manner of inane shite.

For example, Leviticus says if a woman having a period sits on your couch you've got to burn it; it does. And Leviticus says if a man 'knows' your donkey, which means shags but they don't say 'shag' in the bible because 'shag' just sounds like another biblical character, doesn't it—'Shag begat Nob...' So to 'know' means to have sex, you know, which puts a new slant on nodding acquaintances; anyway, if a man 'knows' your donkey, the donkey's got to be put to death; so presum-ably it must have led him on in some way—by having a provocatively short saddle or by saying 'ee-or' when it meant yes.

And of course HIV has done nothing for gays in terms of public relations; a lot of prejudice has been stirred up by HIV. For example, people with HIV cannot get life insurance. The people who most need life insurance can't get it, nor can people who might get HIV or know what it stands for or anybody who might do something that no insurance salesman would ever dream of doing.

And I tried to get life insurance and this little Herbert was sitting there and he said, 'I hope you don't mind me asking Mr Hardy, but have you ever had homosexual relations?'

And I said, 'Well, there was a cousin we used to wonder about, but I couldn't swear to it. Maybe he joined up to learn a trade.'

MARK THOMAS

I reckon the reason why some men are homophobic is because they are frightened. And what they're frightened of is of a bigger bloke than them walking in the pub and going 'Nice arse. Fucking rip me rocket on his ring, look at that.' And they're even more afraid that they'll turn around and go, 'Tee, hee, do you think so?'

EDDIE IZZARD

‘Transvestite. Yes. But I wear what the fuck I want. But I do get a lot of hassle. It's not all roses being a transvestite, you know. A lot of people go, 'Oh, you transvestites, living off the state. Why don't you just go back to Russia?'

A lot of people are jealous as well. They say, 'Oh, I wish I was a transvestite,' and I say, 'Well, if you work hard at school, maybe one day...' But human beings, we really like to gossip, and this is because we like to feel good about ourselves.

And we can do this in two ways; one is a more positive way— you can expend energy, make something, achieve something. Make something out of clay perhaps. You know, a lump of clay, you've seen the people on the telly do it and it's amazing—two fingers, an ornate vase, fifty quid, ta. It looks really piss easy, but you know, it's not that easy. You should never do that in order to chat someone up; never pretend that you can make things out of clay. 'Watch me, I bet I'm fucking good at this [*pottery mime*]...It's a cat factory in fourteenth-century Burundi. Um...fancy a shag?' That's not going to work.

So anyway, that's the more positive method of feeling good about yourself. The second way is gossiping; and you always do negative gossip, it's never positive. It's always, 'Have you heard about so-and-so, oh, everyone hates them. And they really smell at the moment, and they live in a ditch, yes.' This is what we do, so if you're a transvestite, people do tend to gossip. And they do car noises about me, 'VRRRRRRRRM RRRRRRRM.' [*Car noises.*]

So back in the Twenties women put on trousers, we know this, and at that time people said, 'Women can't wear trousers. Back to Russia.' And women said, 'And why not?' And people said, 'Oh...very clever, yes. Quick, run!' And so now women can wear anything. They have total clothing licence—they can wear whatever the fuck they want, and that's great, that's the way it should be.

And so women wear what they want, and so do I. And sometimes I wear trousers. Because people assume, 'Oh, so you've come out, so you should wear a dress all the fucking time.' But no, I wear what the fuck I want. And that's how it works. Boom Boom. Good laugh, but I just wanted to explain, because people think, 'Oh he's not, oh he is, oh...Fuck, I don't care.'

Do get a certain amount of stick though, usually from dickhead men in the street. And they hang out in groups of five, and I've worked this out; it's because they have a fifth of personality each. And they just hang out, shouting, 'Oi! There's a bloke in a dress, bloke in a dress! Hey! Bloke in a dress! Ha, ha!...I told him, yeah.' But they do this to women too; 'Oi, darling! Oi, darling! Ha, ha, ha, ha. I told her. I'm not sure what, but, you know.' I think with women it's bizarre; I think there's some idea that there is a chat-up in there. 'Oi, darling! You and me? You and me, you and me!' I think that if a woman ever did turn round and say, 'OK, let's go now,' that would totally freak them out. They'd go, 'Oh! She said yes. She said fucking yes. I'm not expecting fucking yes. What do I do?' Because you don't go out with someone like that. You'd say, 'What do you want to eat?' And they go, 'Waaaaay! Whoppaaaaa!! Big ones!'

And on some building sites as well. I'm sure there must be some people on the fifth level of building sites, on the fifth level of scaffolding, who are doing the carpentry and the plumbing and stuff like that. But there seems to be about 90 per cent of them who just get up there on the fifth level and just go, 'Fuck-ing hell, he fuck, 'ey, cheese and bananas, oh fucking...oh, she's gone.'

But there's a lot more gay and lesbian people around, and that's very groovy. There's much fewer people who are TV now. I don't know quite why that is, but even gay and lesbian people don't really associate with TVs. They say, 'Yes, we know about them, but we're not sure who they are, erm...they live in a ditch somewhere.'

EDDIE IZZARD

But I've noticed actually since I've come out as being TV that about 80 per cent of the country don't give a monkey's. Eighty per cent of people go, 'Well, you're transvestite, great, but I'm cooking eggs...' And then there's 10 per cent of people who are groovy and out, and working out where sexuality should be. And then there's 10 per cent of people who are really homophobic, who go, 'Grrr...back to Russia...' But as long as they are behind closed doors and don't hurt anyone, I think that's fine.

But fear is very interesting, because coming out is a really scary thing. How to deal with fear. And it's all in your head, it's not out there, it's actually in your head, this is the interesting thing. And I tend to go towards things that really scare me. Not any fucking thing, like leaping off a cliff onto a spike. That scares me, but I don't tend to approach that so much.

But I've also noticed that people react to me in fucking weird ways. Like sometimes you go to newsagents; newsagents see lots of people come in and they have a certain reaction to different people. People looking a bit mean, they go, 'Er, is this person going to nick the till, what's going on?' But a bloke coming in in make-up, I've seen it, they sometimes melt in front of me. Because I come in and they go, 'Ah,' and the signal goes through the brain, and the brain goes, 'No information on this. No information, no information, no information, all around, no fucking information.' And then they start coming out with weird things:

'Get all the toffee crisps out the back, quick!' Toffee crisps? 'Sellotape all the newspapers together. What...what, what, what do you want?!'

And I have to act really quickly here, and I say, 'Er...I want...a bag of crisps! I've got money!'

And they go, 'What, you want crisps? I thought you wanted to shag crisps!'...How very strange.

So anyway, my point is, do come out, it's far more positive, coming out is a great thing, and that's why I did it.

A DIRTY STORY FOR THT
A Short Story by Simon Fanshawe

The sudden appearance of involuntary erections on buses is quite well documented. But not on the Underground. So Michael was shocked by the appearance of one the size of a modest cucumber between Charing Cross and Temple on the Circle Line. He was also shocked because it wasn't his. It belonged to the man sitting opposite. Michael assumed it was involuntary because the man was buried in his book and hadn't seemed to notice it himself.

It looked perfect. Michael watched with a mounting fascination as the man's trousers tightened; the tautness outlining not just his increasingly alluring physical abundance, but the man's underwear too. Boxer shorts. Michael never wore them himself as they never kept him, what his mother had called just after puberty struck, 'tidy'. But he liked them on other men.

The man was beautiful. Bone structure. Slim. Blond. A warning note sounded. Blonds. Michael had seen too many blonds in clubs and on seeing them, wanted to fuck their brains out. But on talking to them, however, he too often discovered that somebody already had. However, this one looked intelligent. And that was Michael's problem.

Michael couldn't help thinking that everyone he fancied was perfect. He was quite capable of seeing someone across the other side of the room, fancying them and, by the time he'd reached them, to have decorated the bedroom, planned the next two holidays and bought the dog. Incurably romantic was the phrase most people used. Cursed was what Michael felt. This so-called romantic attitude blighted his life. It meant that he spent his waking hours falling in love with total strangers and planning their life together, but without ever speaking to them. Anyone. Boys who served him in shops, dispatch riders who arrived in his office, men caught fleetingly in the rear-view mirror of his car as he pulled away from the lights, in fact any male mammal who came within 360 degrees and about 30 yards.

The dreadful paradox was that as soon as he spoke to any of them they inevitably failed to live up to his fantasy. Nobody could be that good. So before he dated them, he left them. In fact for years he had avoided the inconvenience of starting a relationship with anyone. He didn't go out with people, he just split up with them.

So what of the man on the tube with the accidental hard-on? Michael looked carefully at him and decided that the bedroom would be coral. He couldn't quite decide whether they should go abroad this year or next. And as for the dog, he had no idea. But he was in love.

He was also in lust. While he had been weighing up the relative merits of New York versus the Norfolk Broads, he had started to achieve a hardness of his own that was anything but accidental. It too was obvious. Despite it being early in the morning, he was flushed with excitement. And even though the carriage was busy and he was surrounded by people, Michael was more and more consumed with attraction for the blond man with brains. He uncrossed his legs and slouched back a little in the hope that the man might notice his enthusiasm. And he started to stare at the man, taking great care that the man didn't see him doing it.

The man's arms were strong and edible. The pores of his skin were widely spaced and the veins stood out on the back of his slightly hairy hands. Hands were important to Michael. Hands were what turned him on, not just in his mind but physically. Hands were what did the caressing and the stroking. Only tongues did more in love. As he looked the man over, Michael positioned his own hands on the inside of each of his thighs, with his thumbs meeting just across his crotch. Perhaps, if he thought hard enough about the man, the man would sense it and look back. But, much as he wanted the man, he was scared that he might not take his interest as a compliment. So every time he looked at him he casually diverted his eyes as if to show equal interest in the other people in the carriage.

Each time his gaze fixed on the man, Michael's heart actually started to beat faster. Increasingly his body became convinced that the man was the sexiest, most perfect object of desire ever to enter his life. Bravely Michael raised the level of his gaze to the man's eyeline, straining just a little to see his face over the book. This was scary. What if the man stopped reading and caught Michael staring at him? So he looked away again. The man turned the page. As he started to read again, Michael fixed on his face and gently, almost imperceptibly moved his thumbs up and down on the front of his trousers. Now this was daring. In broad tube light, at nine a.m. he was slowly stroking himself for the benefit of the blond brainy stranger with the coral bedroom.

The man went to turn the page again, thought better of it and put his book away. He then clasped his hands together and rested them just below his belt. In the reflection in the window, Michael could see that the man was now directly looking him up and down. The erection may not have been as involuntary as Michael had thought. He looked determinedly away as the man took him in. He didn't dare return his gaze. Michael began to panic now. If he looked at the man, what would he do? Ask him where he wanted to go on holiday next year? Did he like coral? A spaniel?

The man looked at him more and more intently. And Michael got stiffer and stiffer. So did the man. Michael almost plucked up courage to meet his gaze, but as he did so, the man looked away to the ad above Michael's head.

Now it was Michael's turn. Slowly he took in the man's body. Starting with the groin and his slim strong thighs, Michael allowed his stare to wander steadily up to the flat and muscly midriff which was tight against the man's T-shirt, then across his chest, pausing on each clearly visible nipple, to the small curly hairs just poking out of the top. By the time he reached the face, the man had stopped looking at the ad and was looking straight at Michael. Michael blushed and realised that he was still stroking himself. He stopped. The man had no such inhibitions and smiled as he cupped what American porn mags refer to as his 'lunchbox' in his masculine hand. The train pulled into the station. The man stood up. Michael could barely restrain himself from reaching out and unzipping the man's jeans. It wasn't Michael's stop. The man looked down at him and in the crowded carriage smiled a private smile. His eyes twinkled. He was inviting Michael to make it his stop. Michael shook with pleasure, a blush rising to his face along with his own smile.

The train stopped. The doors opened. The man moved towards them, all the time looking back at Michael, fixing him with his whole body, Michael wanted to stand up and go. But now he couldn't make up his mind. Was the man perfect or not? This was decision time. The doors would close any minute. This wasn't a club. He couldn't go back to the man for a second look. How could he be sure about him? The man still looked and Michael still hesitated. His ears were on fire. His adrenalin was up. His heart pumped faster than ever.

The doors were about to close. The man stood with one leg still on the train holding them open. Michael looked at the floor, looked at the man and looked back at the floor. The doors started to close. What to do? Owning up time. Michael leapt up and jumped off the train. He landed on the platform, out of breath from desire, and he gasped at the man, 'Coral?...Spaniels?...What about June in Corfu?' The man paused. 'Couldn't give a toss,' he said, 'but I'd love to suck you off.'

And, do you know? They lived happily ever after.

JULIAN CLARY

sticky members

JULIAN CLARY

I'm actually here to play a game called Sticky Members with you, if you're willing for a shilling? And I can't go any further without my pianist and constant companion. Will you please welcome the very lovely Russell Churney. Good evening, Russell, how are you? [*Enter Russell Churney*]

Russell: Alright.

Julian: Well, that's the main thing. And you do, don't you Russell, remain steadfastly heterosexual?

Russell: Rock solid.

Julian: You've not strayed at all?

Russell: No.

Julian: Why don't you slip off to your instrument now, Russell? Take the weight off your slingbacks. [*Exit Russell to piano.*] And I will also require assistance from my own very glamorous assistant, Mr Hugh Jelly! Hello, Hugh, how are you? [*Enter Hugh Jelly*]

Hugh: I'm very well, sir, thank you.

Julian: Do you like my outfit, Hugh?

Hugh: Yes, it's breathtaking.

Julian: Does it remind you of anybody?

Hugh: Yes, Cilla Black.

Julian: Thank you. You know how to make a 34-year-old homosexual very happy indeed. Could you just outline exactly what your function is this evening, please?

Hugh: Yes. My function this evening is to assist you and agree.

Julian: And what else will we require, Russell, before we go any further?

Russell: We will require an excessively camp backing singer.

Julian: And we have one lurking in the wings: the very lovely Michael Dalton. Good evening, Michael, how are you? [*Enter Michael Dalton*]

Michael: Great mate, bloody bonzo.

Julian: Are you wearing any make-up this evening?

Michael: Yeah, just a touch, yes.

Julian: Maybelline?

Michael: No, it's actually 'Outdoor Girl'.

Julian: And you're an outdoor girl, are you Michael?

Michael: When the mood takes me.

Julian: And the fleet's in. Anyway, Hugh, would you like to tell everyone exactly what is going to happen now?

Hugh: Yes. In a few moments' time, Mr Clary will come amongst you...yes he will, and select two lucky couples to join us up here on stage to play Sticky Members.

Julian: Yes indeed, and I'm looking for couples of any description. You may be a straight couple or a gay couple; you could be an old age pensioner couple or an underage couple. it really doesn't matter, as long as you're coupling. [*Julian walks into audience*] Is this a perm here? Is that a perm?

Woman: I think it might be, yes.

Julian: Nasty. Now, I just have to follow my antennae really, and see where I'm drawn to. Hello, what's your name?

Man: Dominic.

Julian: And who are you here with, Dominic? Your wife? And what's your name?

Woman: Amanda.

Julian: Amanda? And you've had the hairspray out, haven't you, and the curling tongs too? Would you like to play Sticky Members with me, Dominic? What do you do for a living?

Dominic: For my sins, insurance, I'm afraid.

Julian: Oh right, never mind [*walks on*]. Aha, hello, what's your name?

Woman: Karen.

Julian: And you're with...

Man: Andy.

Julian: Andy. What about you two, are you a couple?

Karen: Unfortunately, yes.

Julian: Would you risk it for a biscuit? Could we have some encouragement for them do you think, please? [*audience cheers*] OK, come with me, up you get. Just go round there to the corner of the stage, and Mr Jelly will make you feel at home. [*They go to stage. Julian moves on to find second couple*] Now, hello, what's your name?

Man: Angus.

Julian: Angus? Is that fake tan, or is that natural?

Angus: It's natural.

Julian: And who are you here with? This person here?

Man: Nigel.

Julian: Nigel. And are you a couple? Do you qualify, would you be willing, could I persuade you? Could we have some encouragement. [*Audience cheers. Gay couple follow Julian back onto stage.*] Come with me then. Leave your things behind. [*To Angus*] Oo, you're very tall for your size, aren't you? Have you been to Substation ever, Angus? No? Oh you want to check it out. Very dark lighting. Right, I'll have a chat with you two first, our heterosexual couple, Karen and Andy. Andy, what do you do?

Andy: I'm, er, a tax collector.

Julian: Tax collector. Take a point away please Hugh. And how long have you two been a couple?

Karen: About a year and a half.

Julian: And where did you meet?

Karen: Work.

Julian: Work. Another point away please, Hugh. And do you live together.

Karen: No.

Julian: No? Where do you live then?

Andy: Whitstone, in London.

Julian: Whitstone, I see. Just let your arms hang loosely by your side, that's my advice, Andy. Do you have any pets?

Andy: No, I don't.

Julian: No. Lovely. Over there you go. [*Turning to gay couple*] Come here, Angus and Nigel. How long have you two been a couple?

Nigel: About eight months.

Julian: And where did you meet Nigel, Angus?

Angus: Er...Backstreet.

Julian: Who spoke to who first, can you remember?

Nigel: I think he spoke to me first.

Julian: What did he say?

Nigel: Would you like a white wine?

Julian: Would you like a white wine?[*Laughs in disbelief*]

Hardly Backstreet talk, is it? Are you sure he said wine? And what were you wearing that evening, Nigel?

Nigel: A full leather ensemble.

Julian: And what about you?

Angus: Just in jeans in T-shirt.

Julian: Just casual, take me as you find me. Give them an extra point will you please, Hugh. What we want to do now is find out a little bit about you. Andy, would you like to sit yourself down there? There's nothing to worry about. And Angus, you sit yourself down there. We're going to pop your partners into a soundproof booth now, and wire them up with a Walkman. They'll actually be listening to a Roger Whittaker live album. So you will see the occasional expression of ecstasy flit across their face.

[*Angus and Andy are seated and fitted with headphones so they cannot hear their partners' answers*]

[*To Karen*] Would you like to step in just a little bit closer, keeping your legs wide apart like that as you do so? Would you like someone to hold your hair out of your face for you? Could I say the word Alice band? My questions please, Hugh. First question for you. What colour underwear is your partner wearing?

Karen: Checked.

Julian: Checked? That's not actually a colour as far as I'm aware.

Karen: Blue checked.

Julian: Are they boxers or are they Y-fronts?

Karen: Boxers.

Julian: Blue checked...boxer shorts. Try saying that with a saveloy in your mouth. What about your partner, Nigel, what colour underwear is he wearing?

Nigel: White.

Julian: White? Just plain?

Nigel: Just plain white, yes.

Julian: Are they Y-fronts?

Nigel: Yes.

Julian: Plain white Y-fronts.

Nigel: Yes.

Julian: Clean on today?

Nigel: I would expect so, yes.

Julian: [*To Karen*] Question two: were you attracted to your partner because of (a) his larger-than-life personality, (b) his larger-than-life pay packet, or (c) his larger-than-life penis?

Karen: I've got to go for (c).

Julian: You're going for the penis, I understand. [*Looking at Andy*] Who'd have thought? [*To Nigel*] Same for you about Angus, was it the personality you liked, or the pay packet or just the penis?

Nigel: Oh definitely the penis, yes.

Julian: The penis. OK, fair enough. Could we release the partners now please, and er, we'll compare their answers, and see what they have to say? [*Andy and Angus are released and rejoin their partners.*] And could we have the gags, please? Would you mind slipping that over you so that you can't cheat at all? [*Karen and Nigel are gagged.*] That's actually a gag there, OK? [*To Angus*] I'm sure you've seen one of those before. [*To Andy*] Could you tell me please, what colour underwear are you wearing?

Andy: Green.

Julian: And what sort of pattern is that?

Andy: I think it's check.

Julian: Green check. Boxers or Y-fronts?

Andy: Boxers.

Julian: OK, well, we were actually told blue, so I'll have to give you half a mark there. Same question for you Angus, what have you got underneath these extra long-leg jeans you're wearing?

Angus: White – they're sort of white boxers, white shorts.

Julian: Right, I'll have to give you half a point as well. Do you think your partner was attracted to you because of your larger-than-life personality, your larger-than-life pay packet, or your larger-than-life penis?

Andy: [*Silence*]

Julian: Did you hear the question? Pay packet, personality or penis.

Andy: Pay packet.

Julian: Well, you knew it couldn't be personality. But sadly, no, it was the penis that we were told. Same for you Angus, was it personality back there in Backstreet, eight long months ago, pay packet or penis?

Angus: I'm going to be immodest and say penis.

Julian: Is the right answer. Full marks there. Could we have the scores now please, Hugh?

Hugh: Yes indeed, the scores are: the straight couple have minus one and a half, and the nancy boy couple have three and a half.

Julian: Well, commiserations to you, and congratulations to you. It's funny how things work out, isn't it? But in this strange showbusiness world where we live, you will get more or less the same prizes. [*Hands each flowers, T-shirts, condoms and a 'Fanny the Wonderdog' statuette. Couples exit.*]

sexual
advice

*WENDY HAD BEEN TAUGHT NEVER TO TRUST BOYS,
AND TO ALWAYS TAKE HER OWN PRECAUTIONS*

GAYLE TUESDAY

Now, I've got this weekly column in the *Daily Star* where I give out beauty tips and everything. And my beauty tip for this week, girls, is how to look slimmer at parties. Now, my advice is that you must wear black, and then stand all night in front of a black background. Now, some people might argue that you look like a little fat head with no body at all...but you're more likely to get a shag, and that's what counts. Now, I get a lot of letters from girls saying, 'Dear Gayle, I've been invited to this party, but I've put on half a stone. I'm two stone overweight as it is. All the other girls who are going to be at the party are going to be thinner than me. All the boys are going to fancy all the other girls...' And what I always say to these girls who write in with this terrible, terrible low self-esteem...best not go to the party. You'll only upset yourself...and you'll spoil it for the others.

PAUL CALF

A quick word for the lads: seduction. It's an art form. You can't just say, 'Hello darling, fancy a shag?' You've got to say, 'Please'. You've got to sweet-talk them: 'Hello. What's your name? My name's Paul. Do you fancy a shag? Please.' And don't, for fuck's sake, forget their name. Write it down if you have to. On their back if you have to. I always keep a felt-tip pen by the bed just in case. Talk to them while you're having sex, be polite, you know: 'Would you tickle my balls, please? Would you like me to suck your tits?' Start a dialogue.

PAULINE CALF

Hey, but listen, lads, if you try to seduce a woman, right, if you take her back to your place, be sophisticated. Put a bit of light music on...Carpenters or something like that. Lower the lights, take your socks off. You know, little

▶ 140 things like that make all the difference. If you nip into the toilet, while you're in there, rinse your nob out in the sink. A clean penis might just tip the balance, do you know what I mean?

JO BRAND

Now you might have worked out that I'm a bit crap at seducing people. I think it's because there's no sexy underwear in my size really. The nearest thing you get to sexy underwear is something without a length of tarpaulin in the gusset. So I have to have a lot of sexual fantasies. And my favourite one is smearing my naked body with chocolate and cream...and then just being left on my own to eat it. But on the very rare occasions I do actually get a bloke in a room on his own, it just seems too good an opportunity to miss just to punch him in the fucking gob, quite honestly.

So, crap at seduction, but hopefully in the future modern science might be able to do something for me. Because I read recently in a journal that apparently, six scientists have managed to get an ape and a pig together genetically and produce a creature that can peel a banana with its trotters. Apparently, Lazio have expressed an interest. Gazza, broke his legs. Sad old fucker.

MARK LAMARR

I've been single for a long time, because I don't get on with people. My last girlfriend had a nickname for me; she used to call me 'kitten'. And I hated that, because I just thought that it didn't really suit me. But apart from that, it's not really one of those nicknames where you can do one back. You can't go, 'Oh, cat,' – it sounds really stupid. You can't go 'dog', definitely. So, she used to call me 'kitten' all the time. And then we split up and I found out afterwards (because she told my friends) that it was because my breath smelt like cat food.

SPITTING
IMAGE

Spitting Image

Alastair Burnett: [*off stage*] Aha, Aha! Ladies and gentlemen, there now follows a special Royal Command performance of 'Sex Talk'. Will you please rub your hands together gleefully and say 'Goody, goody, an excuse for some gratuitous titillation.'

Queen: Good evening, loyal subjects, and welcome to 'Sex Talk'. Now, I would like to warn the panel that although this should be an open and frank discussion of sexual matters, we have been asked that under no circumstances should we use the following sexual swearwords: 'fuck, bollocks, prick, cocksucking, and wanker'.

John Major: Excuse me – I think someone has accidentally given you my memo to Michael Portillo.

Queen: Oh. I am so sorry. Now, with one on the panel is firstly, a leading Tory that it is my duty to see once a week for ten minutes...

Prince Philip: Good evening.

Queen: No not you, Philip, it's John Major.

Major: Good evening, Sir Robin.

Queen: Next to him is an outspoken man who has never tried to hide his taste for guns and pornography, and whose numerous affairs with young actresses are legendary...

Philip: Good evening.

Queen: No, no, not you Philip, it's Michael Winner.

Michael Winner: Hello, sexy.

Queen: And finally, the man who has been my constant sexual companion for the last 40 years...

Philip: Well that can't be me!

Queen: Shut up, Philip. Let's get on to our first question, which is from Mr Derek Rodwell, who is a female impersonator...

Female in Audience: What does the panel think is the secret of a long and happy relationship?

Queen: Mmmm. John Major?

Major: Well, my secret is to keep things spicy and exciting in the bedroom. For example, sometimes I'll turn the light out before I take my underpants off. It drives Norma wild and gives her amazing orgasms.

Winner: How do you know?

Major: She makes those orgasmic noises women make, you know, sort of [*shuts eyes and does snoring noise*].

Queen: That's not an orgasm!

Philip: Isn't it? Bloody hell, now she tells me.

Queen: Michael Winner?

Winner: I believe that having frequent sex makes couples stick together.

Philip: It does if you don't have any tissues.

Winner: Why do you think Princess Anne and Mark Phillips split up?

Queen: Just good luck really...Now, I think we should get on with the next question from the audience. Woman at the front.

Woman: My daughter is nearly ten years old. When should she learn about sex?

Queen: Her daughter is ten years old. When should she learn about sex?

Winner: Tell you what – wait till she's sixteen and send her round to my place.

Queen: Personally, I think a well-balanced, mature youngster could probably be told at around six or seven.

Philip: As for Edward, we still haven't told him.

Queen: Yes, and we should have been more frank with Charles.

Philip: What do you mean? Thanks to me he now has perfectly normal sexual habits, like ringing up married women and saying he wants to be their tampon.

Queen: John Major – coming to you, er, as it were, what did you tell your children about things like, say, fellatio?

Major: Er – fellatio. I – I, well, you know, I told them a bit.l

Queen: What exactly?

Major: Well I – er – I told them about him being a – er – philosopher?

Winner: Philosopher??

Major: Er, I mean, recipe. Italian recipe.

Winner: You don't know what you're talking about, you impotent little necrophiliac!

Major: Flattery will get you nowhere, Michael.

Queen: Right, let's have another question from the audience.

Woman: Does the panel think that pornography has a bad effect on men's attitudes to sex?

Queen: Mmm. Michael Winner.

Winner: Well, I've studied all these pornographic films and magazines very carefully, very carefully indeed.

Queen: And?

Winner: No – that's it...

Queen: Well, I think they should ban all pornographic magazines. Especially that dreadful one with photos of Readers' Wives.

Philip: Look, I didn't know they were going to print it.

Major: Norma likes to use magazines in our lovemaking. She reads out bits whilst I make love to her.

Winner: Really? Which magazines?

Major: You know, *TV Quick, Gardening World...*

Philip: It's the hardcore stuff I don't like – what was that disgusting picture the servants have up on their wall, dear? You know, the woman baring everything, the man virtually copulating with her, bosoms everywhere. What was that?

Queen: That was Fergie in the *Sunday Mirror*, Philip.

Philip: Bloody servants, if they're not shagging Anne, they're nicking things...

Queen: That reminds me, Philip, good news. The police have recovered some of the stuff that got stolen from our bedroom.

Philip: The painting?

Queen: No, the other stuff! [*Holds up S & M Mask.*] You know. Your whip and rubber mask.

Philip: Er, yes, dear, very nice, now put it away.

Queen: [*Holds up vibrator*] And I never thought I'd see this old friend again.

Major: Oh, you've got one of those novelty cocktail stirrers, the same as Norma's.

Philip: Quick, somebody draw the curtains. Er – that's all from this Royal Sex Talk.

Queen: And remember, everyone, always wear a condom. If you don't wear a condom, you might end up with dreadful children like mine.

All: Bye!!!!!!

A SHORT STORY
by Steve Punt

It was, as I recall, in the winter of 1892 that my friend Sherlock Holmes and I became embroiled in one of the most singular cases we were ever called upon to deal with. Holmes had been idle ever since his success with unravelling the conundrum of the Unshaven Chemist, and apart from assisting in the recovery of the Figgis-Snetterton Plans (thus saving for Britain the patent on the most advanced kitchen ventilation equipment then available) and solving the labyrinthine complexities surrounding the murder of Sir Roger Parkes (the naval attaché found with navel attached to a ship's propeller off Finisterre) he had been in a state of indolent melancholy

*GOD SHOWED ADAM WHAT HE'D HAVE TO USE
UNTIL HE'D CREATED EVE*

all autumn. 221b Baker Street was a sorry apartment indeed as the strains of Holmes' violin filled the air – slow, lugubrious Bach when my friend was thinking, until a frenetic burst of Rimsky-Korsakov would announce that he had once again been at his cocaine.

One evening I arrived back at 221b to find our landlady showing a woman around the hall. The woman was unknown to me, but her countenance was pleasing, not to say handsome.

'Ah, Dr Watson,' began the landlady, with whom I had not spoken recently, following a slight altercation over Holmes' use of various fixtures and fittings as weapons in subduing Josiah Madd at the conclusion of the Adventure of the Psychopathic Newsagent. 'Pray, let me introduce Miss Marilyn Worstenholme. She and a companion will henceforth be renting 221c Baker Street. I hope and trust that you and Mr Holmes will prove yourselves good neighbours.'

Holmes was pacing the study when I arrived, clutching his violin in an agitated state.

'It is a source of great disappointment to me, Watson,' he cried, 'that the violin is perceived by the public as such a high-flown instrument, beloved only of the highly cultured, and sneered at by the masses. Surely it would be possible to popularise it? Someone could be found – someone who, if necessary, could feign a Cockney accent, spike their hair and talk with a lisp?...' His eyes sparkled, but dimmed again. 'No – it is a ridiculous notion, Watson. Now – have you brought me any decent shit?'

'I have not,' I replied, with dignity. 'Your dependence on artificial stimulants is something which I, as a doctor...'

'Oh, fiddlesticks, Watson!' came the reply. 'Pray, do not lecture me. I am not a weight-lifter. Crime detection is not an occupation which must be subject to such prudery.'

'If the Lord had intended us to use drugs...'

'If the Lord had not intended us to use drugs, my dear Watson, he would have made a world which was bearable without them. But let us desist from such wrangling. How goes the metropolis? What nefarious capers require my talents? Which sordid manifestations of human wickedness need my utmost attention?'

'You mean, has anyone been bumped off today?'

'Indeed, Watson, you have hit the nail so squarely on the head as to drive it clean through the wood and out the other side. Has anyone been bumped off today? Is the capital littered with corpses? Are its streets and thoroughfares blocked with stiffs? For nothing could make me happier.'

'I'm afraid not,' I said. 'No murders today.'

'Ah,' said Holmes. 'It is an evil sign of the times, Watson, a symptom of an enfeebled and decadent zeitgeist, when the homicides cease. All great, healthy, powerful societies are full of murders. Think through history. The Roman Empire – murders galore. Renaissance Italy – deaths aplenty. Elizabethan England – safe? Tell that to Christopher Marlowe. Revolutionary France – they were dropping like flies. Even our own age, the zenith of Empire, had been accompanied by numerous slayings which attest to the spirit, cunning and drive of a great people. Think of the mental agility required of a great poisoner, the guts and strength needed to accomplish a stabbing – these are the qualities that made us great, Watson. I fear for England when its citizens no longer seethe with the desire to put strychnine in each other's cocoa.'

'I believe you need a rest, Holmes,' I said. 'You are talking almost treasonably. All murderers are fiends fit only for the gallows.'

'It is for your liberal opinions that I value you so highly, Watson,' replied Holmes. 'For you must understand that murder is my livelihood. I depend on it, as the publican depends on beer.'

'Well, I am afraid that there have been no murders of late, and I, for one, rejoice in it.'

'Then my mind remains idle, Watson, and shall do so until someone is found spattered all over the London-Brighton line, or dangling from Admiralty Arch with a carrot up each nostril.' (Holmes' astonishing premonitory powers were to be proved the following year, when we found ourselves drawn into the Adventure of the Man Found Dangling From Admiralty Arch with a Carrot Up Each Nostril.)

My friend stalked the room for a while, clearly upset that none of London's citizens had met a grisly end and provided him with something to do. Neither of us realised, however, that events were about to begin which would provide a far more singular investigation that any murder we had ever encountered.

It began later that same night. It was getting fairly late, and I was preparing to retire to bed, although Holmes was busy setting up some test tubes and retorts for a chemical experiment he wanted to conduct. Suddenly both of us were aware of a low, moaning noise, slightly indistinct. It sounded like an animal at first, but as we attuned our ears, the noise became recognisably human.

'What on earth is that, Holmes?'

'Very singular, Watson,' replied my friend. 'It sounds indubitably like a man in some pain, and it appears to be emanating from upstairs.'

'But there are only two ladies upstairs,' I replied. 'Miss Worstenholme and her companion.'

'Most odd,' replied Holmes. 'Anyway, Watson, I must continue with this experiment.' So saying, he took a large pair of scissors, and cut one of his shirts clean in two.

'Whatever are you doing, Holmes?'

'Ah, you may well enquire, Watson. You see, ordinary powders leave behind the really stubborn stains at forty degrees, so I intend washing one half of the shirt in our normal powder, but the other half in concentrated nitric acid.'

I did not follow this at all, so I said goodnight and went to bed. Before I went to sleep I thought I could hear more groans from upstairs, but I was so tired that I was asleep before I could be sure.

It was a couple of days later that the dung really hit the fan, as we used to say in the Army. Holmes and I were consuming an excellent breakfast when Holmes looked up from the morning paper with a grave look in his eye.

'The foul breath of scandal looks set to afflict the nation's nose,' he said. 'Look at this on the front page of the *Daily Bulletin*.'

He handed me the journal, and I perused the story which Holmes had indicated. It ran thus—

'TITTLE-TATTLE OF MINISTER'S MISDOINGS—All Westminster is currently agog with Rumour concerning a Minister of the crown, whose identity is currently a closely-contrived Secret, and shall remain so on Our Part, though other, most scurrilous publications shall doubtless venture the Name, baseless though the allegations against him are said to be. The Allegations in question, baseless though they are, do not need to be enumerated here for more Public titillation, but as a matter of record it is our Duty to set them down. It appears that the Minister in question has on sundry and diverse occasions of late been in the company of Ladies of questionable Virtue from whom he has received Certain Services, which it is not in the nature of this newspaper to divulge. The Minister in question has denied all the allegations, which are in any case Baseless.'

'Good heavens, Holmes!' I expostulated. 'Who would have thought it?'

'I suspect the work of agitators,' muttered Holmes. 'Agents of the Kaiser, or of some Balkan power intent on making mischief. I suspect, Watson, that here may be a case at last which will exercise my mental muscles to their fullest capacity.'

This thought excited Holmes so much that he abandoned his eggs and gammon and returned to his chemical bench, there to examine the results of the previous night's experiment.

'It is as I suspected, Watson,' he cried after examining the two halves of shirt. 'You see? With the normal powder those really stubborn stains remain——you see there, some blood, a relic of the Adventure of the Haemophiliac Knife-Grinder, and down there are some spatters of Devonshire mud remaining from our little tussle at the end of the Adventure of the Irritating Rambler. But see here! With concentrated nitric acid the stains have vanished.'

'True, Holmes,' I said. 'But so has the shirt.'

'Precisely, Watson. From this we can learn something of acid-bath murderers, but quite what we can learn, I do not know. Now—to business.'

For the rest of the day Holmes sat in his favourite armchair, slumped in thought. Around mid-afternoon, a knock came at the door.

'Aha!' cried Holmes, rising instantly. 'A client! At last! Someone with some appalling problem for me to solve!'

I rushed to open the door, and there stood a small, middle-aged man who wore spectacles and slightly shabby clothing.

'Come in, dear sir!' cried Holmes. 'Don't tell me. Wife disappeared? Wife murdered? Are you receiving death threats? Whatever it is, come in and tell me all about it.'

The gentleman seemed unwilling to step inside, and stared about him somewhat sheepishly.

'Er—are you Babette?' he said.

'Quite wrong,' cried Holmes.

'Is this the right address for..services?'

'Indeed!' I beamed. 'Mr Holmes here is too modest to admit it, but his services have been employed by some of the crowned heads of Europe.'

This seemed to shock the man, and his jaw fairly dropped.

'Really?' he cried.

'Oh yes,' I continued. 'Many a great personage has made their way to Baker Street, and left fully satisfied.'

'Really, Watson, you flatter me too much,' said Holmes. 'Invite the gentleman in, for in truth, sir, it is some time since we had a client.'

The chap now seemed extremely flustered. 'This is 221c Baker Street?' he asked.

'No, no,' I replied, a trifle annoyed. 'This is 221b. Flat C is upstairs.'

'Thank Christ for that,' said the man. I was shocked by his profanity. He blushed a deep red and then scampered upstairs.

'This is all distinctly odd, Watson,' said Holmes, obviously disappointed at having been let down. 'For did you not tell me that the occupant upstairs is called Marilyn Worstenholme? Then who is this Babette?'

'Evidently that must be her companion,' I replied.

'That is distinctly odd, Watson. The name would suggest a French lady, and I would venture to suggest that our good landlady would be unlikely to let out one of her rooms to a foreigner.'

Our discussion was interrupted at this point by the arrival of the first edition of the evening paper, and the front page was full of further news of the scandal.

'I have been distracted from this by our strange visitor, Watson. I must direct my thoughts back to this poor Minister, whose career, it seems, is so endangered by sinister middle-European forces.'

As Holmes pondered the problem I happened to glance through the window, and noticed a hansom cab pulling up in the street outside.

'Good heavens, Holmes!' I cried, as I espied the personage disembarking therefrom. 'You were correct!'

Holmes rushed to the window and we watched as a certain Minister of the Crown in Her Majesty's Government paid off the driver of the hansom, and, with an anxious glance around him, headed towards our front door.

'It is as I thought,' said Holmes. 'The poor man is coming here to consult with me. Make ready, Watson—I dare say he will be in quite a state.'

I plumped a few cushions and checked all the decanters, and the two of us listened as the tread upon the stair grew louder. It then grew softer.

'That is very strange,' I commented. 'He appears to be going upstairs.'

'Most singular,' said Holmes. 'Perhaps he has mistaken the address.'

But apparently, no mistake had been made, for the Minister did not return to our floor. We heard the door upstairs open, and then all was silence.

'All rather curious, Watson,' said Holmes, once again disappointed in his hope that his keen brain might be required.

It was a few minutes later that the strange groaning began once again.

'Listen!' cried Holmes.

I listened, and my blood ran cold. For from upstairs were emanating the unmistakable sounds of a fearsome beating. The moans were louder than ever.

'I was right, Watson!' whispered Holmes. 'This Miss Worstenholme is obviously nothing more than a front for some sinister Eastern European subversives. Even now one of our country's senior Ministers is being tortured! Who knows what state secrets he may divulge! Quickly!'

With this Holmes ran from the room. I took my trusty pistol from its box and followed him upstairs. Holmes was crouched outside the door to 221c.

'Listen, Watson! The fiends! They have already wrung from him the name of the Head of Overseas Intelligence!'

Sure enough, from within could be heard moans of 'Moore, Moore.' Only three people in the whole country knew that Sir Nicholas Moore was the Head of Overseas Intelligence—the Prime Minister, the Foreign Secretary, and Sherlock Holmes. (The Queen had not been told, as the FO felt that having been married to a German made her a security risk.)

'This is intolerable,' muttered Holmes. 'Stand back, Watson, and be ready with your pistol.'

With this, he laid his shoulder against the door and with a mighty shove we found ourselves inside the apartment. The sight which greeted our eyes will stay with me forever. Miss Worstenholme and her companion were standing, both in bizarre apparel consisting largely of belts, and both were clutching horse-whips. The Minister, for his part, was lying on a strange contraption which seemed to be some sort of frame. His ankles and wrists had been shackled to the frame, and he was entirely unclothed apart from a school tie around his neck and a small dunce's cap perched on his head.

'What is the meaning of this?' cried Holmes.

'What are you doing?' said Miss Worstenholme, turning to

face us. She was sporting a pair of highly polished riding-boots and, I noticed for the first time, in her shock at the door being opened, a mortar-board had fallen from her head.

'What the devil are you playing at, you idiots? Shut the bloody door!' cried the Minister, his face beetroot-red.

'Do not panic,' said Holmes. 'My friend Dr Watson and I will have you free in no time, and these villains will be safely in the hands of Inspector Lestrade.'

'Lestrade? Isn't he due at nine-thirty?' said Miss Worstenholme. Holmes and I exchanged puzzled glances.

'Do not worry, sir,' said Holmes to the Minister. 'We will have you free in no time at all.'

'Piss off!' responded the Minister. 'For heaven's sake—ten guineas this cost me.'

'Which of you is Babette?' I asked.

'Babette?' said the Minister. 'You told me your name was Nicole.'

Miss Worstenholme walked across to a small table, her assorted leather garments creaking noisily as she did so. From the table she picked up a card, which she handed to me.

'My card,' she said.

I glanced at it. It read 'Naughty Boys Need Strict Mistress. West End. Telephone 23.'

'You have a telephone?' I asked.

'Been a boon, love,' replied Miss Worstenholme's companion.

'Do I understand,' said Holmes, 'that gentlemen pay to be strapped to this contraption and struck with whips?'

'That's right.'

'Very singular. Come, Watson. I need to think.'

We returned downstairs, and Holmes lit a pipe. After a few minutes in which he puffed his way into a miasma of smoke, he spoke.

'Let us consider the facts, Watson. Firstly, there are reports of an incipient scandal at Westminster. Secondly, a Cabinet Minister appears at 221 Baker Street, apparently to consult me about this problem. Half an hour later he is discovered upstairs, shackled, obviously in some pain, and yet most unwilling to be rescued from his predicament. What conclusions can we draw?'

I hesitated, but Holmes did not wait for my reply.

'Send a telegram to the editor of the *Daily Flysheet*, Watson. Telegram to read—MP'S VICE DEN SHOCKER STOP CALL GIRL TELLS ALL STOP HE TOLD ME NEVER TO STOP STOP.' I looked at Holmes, bemused, but he just grinned.

'The thing about us Victorians, Watson,' he said, 'is that we weren't as stupid as everyone thinks.'

drink &
drugs

PAUL CALF

You've got to be very careful when you bring a girl back to your house. 'Cause if you're both pissed, you've got to be careful, so what I do is I get them to sign a contract; a sexual contract. This is what she has to sign, if she's going to have sex with me:

I,... (NAME) being of sound mind, and not a bad body, agreed to have a shag with Mr Paul Calf on his settee/back of car, on my back, on top and doggy and all other positions to be mutually agreed upon.

....
Signed

small print
I also agree that when Paul has come/passed out, to sleep on the wet patch.

ARTHUR SMITH

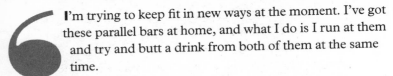

I'm trying to keep fit in new ways at the moment. I've got these parallel bars at home, and what I do is I run at them and try and butt a drink from both of them at the same time.

Of course, the Seventies is all the fashion now. I'll let you into a little secret: in the Seventies I actually won Young Scientist of the Year. Yeah, he was a nice little lad... You know, he used to stay up in the attic with his test tubes and that, he was nice.

And I got invited recently to a Seventies party, and I got quite excited and got out my plastic mac, my Cat Stevens LP and the shoes, and I got there and it turned out it was a party for people in their seventies, and tragically they didn't even notice that I was gatecrashing, and I was pissed off about that.

Met my granddad there, who, in common with all old people, gets up at half past four in the morning. So, I said, you know, 'Grandad, what do you do at half past four in the morning?' And he said, 'Well, you know, Caroline,' because he likes to call me that for some reason, he said, 'You have a cup of tea, and a piece of toast and before you know, it's half past five!'

I miss the old-style parties. The parties I go to these days, it's all bloody Perrier and babies. Real parties, that's what I remember: two pints of Valpolicella, chunder in the garden, eight-mile walk home. Maybe a fight if you're lucky, cop off with somebody's grandmother.

Just a word about drugs. Nice.

ARTHUR SMITH

ARTHUR SMITH

This is an impression of three things [*holds both arms aloft*] firstly, an over-enthusiastic nazi; secondly, Mark Thatcher; but mainly, this is an impression of a drunk having a piss. It's actually a little bit sexist, that, because quite obviously, a female would have to be in a right state to be having a piss like that.

Flying is another thing I'm not a big fan of. You have to be if you're a comedian because then you can do a routine about it. But I've found a way of dealing with my fear of flying and that is to upset the other passengers more than you.

So when you hear the Captain say 'Good evening everybody, this is Captain Robinson here,' you shout out, 'Oh no, not him! Not old shaky Robinson! I didn't know he flew during opening hours!'

And then when they are running through the safety instructions, ask questions. Like, 'Excuse me, what happens if a hole blows in the top of the aeroplane and people start getting sucked out? Are you going to turn on the no-smoking sign? Because I'll definitely be needing a fag if that happens...'

Well, it's near the end of the gig, so 've put me going home gear on now, you see. No, actually, I bought this off of a bloke in Balham market, he reckoned it was the Turin shroud. It's quite kind of funny if you wear it inside out and round the wrong way, I tell you.

RHONA CAMERON

If you're drinking a lot tonight and planning to have sex, this is a mistake. Drinking and sex don't go. Because what happens is that you go out—bit of music, bit of entertainment—you have thirty pints of lager, and you meet someone. And for some stupid reason, you think that sex might be a good idea.

And then you get home with them and you think, 'What the fuck have I done? It's two in the morning, I'm in a room, I've never been here, it's dark, I can't find anything, I don't know this person...' And suddenly, sex becomes 'The Crystal Maze'.

I'm in the room, what should I be looking for? How long have I got? There's a hole here but I don't...' And somebody goes, 'Come on, you've only got thirty seconds, put it in your mouth, try that.'

'No, never liked that, what shall I do? Is there an opening? How long?'

'Twenty seconds, go in from behind.'

'I can't find that water.'

'It's down there, come on, ten seconds. There's the Yellow Pages, phone a taxi and leave. Got the taxi? Get out, get out, get out! Yes!'

RHONA CAMERON

'I was thinking about my parents. They've grown up with me, obviously, and they don't get shocked by me any more. I can tell my mum and dad anything about my life, and it doesn't bother them.

I can say, 'Yes, Mum, I have tried the controversial drug, Ecstasy,' and she says, 'That's fine,' and I can say, 'Yes, I have been drunk and shown my vagina at parties,' and Mum says, 'That's OK, I did too as a young woman growing up in the Forties, so did your gran, and her mum before that, so don't you worry.'

But there is one thing, one fucking thing that I have to lie about to my parents when I go home, and that is smoking. 'Do you smoke?' 'No, no, I just smell of smoke, because someone smoked in the taxi.' I'm 28! It's ridiculous. They're so obsessed by it. All the time they phone me up, 'You're not smoking, are you?'

So I've got this fantasy in my head that my mum and dad are at home and they're sitting in the family living room, and just for the purpose of this joke a pornographic film comes on the television…and I'm in it. So mum says, 'Bill, is that our Rhona getting shagged up the bum there?'

And my dad comes in from the kitchen – because he's middle-aged and he's been cleaning out these tupperware boxes really sadly and slowly, hasn't he? And they stick little labels on them saying 'nuts' and 'raisins'. You can fucking see through them, you don't need labels. So Dad comes wandering through and he goes, 'Yes, Jean, I think that is our Rhona getting shagged up the bum there…That's not a fucking cigarette she's got in her mouth though, is it?'

IAN COGNITO

You're going to want to know about my fucking sex life, aren't you? Well, I'll tell you this, I've got two kids, that's the truth of the matter, and the latest one, little William, and he's tiny and I fucking love him; I could just chop him up and snort him through a five pound note.

Mind you, don't take drugs all the time. It's all very clever us comedians saying take loads of drugs; DO NOT take drugs all the time, alright...'cause like my mum used to say to me, you won't feel the benefit of them when you go out.

PAUL CALF

If I'm in a good mood, I'm going to go to a club later on. It's a fucking great club; free drinks all night and a guaranteed shag at the end of it. I've not been, but my sister went last week.

LILY SAVAGE

Do you know, I'm getting a cold, and I came in here about two o'clock in the afternoon, I felt like shit. And one of the band gave me a Beecham's powder. I never knew that you chopped it up on a mirror and sniffed it through a five pound note.

GREG PROOPS

Sex isn't a priority for you guys. We ought to make a book about what is a priority, and that would be drinking. I have never been to a place where people drink this much, man. Y' all drink like someone is going to take

it away from you. I can't believe that you're all sitting so quietly now, just knowing there's a pub open somewhere. The French drink to be social, Americans drink to have a good time...British people drink so that they can projectile vomit on a statue.

MARK LAMARR

There was something I meant to mention earlier that's very important, not a safety announcement, but a legal requirement. There are signs up as you enter the building saying, 'Anyone caught using or selling illegal drugs will be dealt with by the Management'.

And it's important not just from the legal side; I don't know if you know, but last year twelve young people lost their lives due to Ecstasy. Now I don't know about you, but to me that sounds like...quite a nice way to go. Just given the choice, that's all I'm saying. Given the choice, Cancer/Ecstasy.

There was a film about that plane crash in the Andes, and some people went down and were probably half burnt to death, with broken limbs. And they were there for ages and had to drink their own piss for quite a long time, and then eat their dead friends until eventually there were no dead friends left, and they died of starvation out there in the wasteland...or ecstasy. Given the choice, that's all I'm saying.

So 'Anyone caught using or selling illegal drugs will be dealt with by the Management', and underneath, it says 'Just say no'. Vitally important, that; whenever any of the Management come up to you and say, 'Are you using or selling illegal drugs?', just say no, that keeps them happy.

sex

JEFF GREEN

'We should have had six months on foreplay at school, shouldn't we? I'm as bad as everyone else, I skip it. It's too hard, isn't it? We've got a time difference, that's the problem, isn't it? 'Cause women need bloody ages, don't they? Like, minutes sometimes. It's too long, 'cause most men go, 'Well, I'm ready; 0.7 seconds, my fastest yet.'

I was thinking of going celibate. I had this really horrible experience with sex. It actually put me off it for the rest of my life. Have you ever had that one where you actually see your face as you're having an orgasm? And you just think, 'Never, ever again, you ugly bastard.' The worst thing was it wasn't in a mirror...it was in a shop window.

And I actually think women have a much better time sexually than men. Because you've got all the orgasms, haven't you? I've read it in *Cosmopolitan*: 'You're entitled to as many orgasms as you want'. Men fear *Cosmopolitan* coming out. They think, 'What the fuck are they going to make us do this week? Have you seen the front cover?' 'Yeah, yoghurt. I don't even like yoghurt on its own.' We're up for most things but...Petit Filou's quite nice, I suppose.

But men don't complain about their orgasms. How many do we get? We get one which knocks us out in case we want another one. And she's going, 'Hey, that was quite nice, any chance of anoth...?' Zzzzzzzzzzzz (snore). Eight hours. And women have got all the best noises sexually. You've got seagull noises. They're lovely. What have men got? A bloody wart hog breaking cover. We got the shit end of the stick on the noises front, didn't we? 'I'm coming, ha, ha, aaaaaaaaah, ah, zzzzzzzzzzzzz.'

GAYLE TUESDAY

Obviously, along with all my topless work, I've done quite a lot of television. I was on 'The Word', my first appearance ever. But I didn't really feel comfortable, you know. All those intellectual types, like Amanda de Cadanet. You know, all superior. But I ain't joking, when I did it the cameraman was really trying to get off with me, you know. So I thought I'd confront him with it. So I went straight up to him and I said, 'You want to shag me, don't you?' And he said, 'Is the Pope Catholic?' So I said, 'Don't change the subject.' I'm no fool.

PAUL CALF

I remember the last time I had sex with my girlfriend, Julie. I was about to come, and right on coming, she said, 'No Paul, don't come. Think of Esther Rantzen.' I shot my fucking load. Still, that's life.

RHONA CAMERON

I was thinking about when I first had sex; I lost my virginity to my next-door neighbour when I was about sixteen. In fact it's very disturbing for me, because the memory I have to live with for the rest of my life is that the man that I lost it to was actually wearing white socks at the time...and a pink Pringle jumper and a shaggy wet perm. I think his name was Kevin Keegan. I come from Mosselborough in Scotland, where there's nothing else to do except have sex. It's just full of little Scottish people wandering around in string vests going, 'That'll be my teatime.' So I thought, I've got to get out of Mosselborough, so what I'll do, I'll pass my 'O' level French because then you get to go on an exchange trip. Which was great because I got to go to Paris, which is beautiful, and then some poor sad French person had to come to fucking Mosselborough. She was wandering around in a little stripy top and kagoul going, 'Rhona, what is there to do?' I said, 'Well, you can shag the neighbour if you want, but it's already been done. Fucking boring as well.'

IAN COGNITO

I don't have sex any more, I've given it up. 'Cause I've been living with my woman for seven years now, and when you've been living with someone for that long, sex goes out the window. Well fuck it, I'll do it anywhere to make it more interesting. And we were lying in bed together the other night, she was picking the blackheads out my back and I was gobbing up blood into a pair of my old pants and she said to me, 'Ian, whatever happened to that handsome, virile man I used to live with, that sexy man who used to make love to me on the spin dryer – while it was on with an unbalanced load; on the rug, in front of the telly, hallway, staircase, anywhere, any time of the day?' I said, 'I kicked the fucker out, he wasn't doing his washing up. Why should I stand for that?'

But when she saw I was hurt she had to admit that although I'm 35 years old (and I know I don't look it), that I can still make love like an 18-year-old. *Yes*, 35 years old, still doing it like an 18-year-old... Get it over with quick, get up to the pub and tell your mates about it.

GREG PROOPS

I find it kind of ironic to be invited to talk to an English crowd about sex... Kind of like talking to an American crowd about reading, isn't it? Or an Italian crowd about law and order. I think you get the drift. English people and sex. Sex isn't really a priority here, is it? I can't get anyone to look me in the eye on the fucking train here, much less shag me.

BEN ELTON

We've all been asked to talk about sex, and I feel slightly that we should have defined what we mean by sex. Because it seems to me there are basically two types of sex in the world: there's real sex, which we all do, which is a bit bony, a bit knobbly, a bit floppy, and then there's the media sex where everything is firm and everything's hard. And unfortunately the sex we do alone, we think that's just us, and we share the media sex with everybody else and we think, 'Jesus, that's what everybody else does, everybody's so good at it.'

It's like a conspiracy, it's exploitable. People's sexual drives are exploited. Like these telephone sex lines. It cannot work. Exploiting people's loneliness for profit. I mean, it can't work. If you were hungry, would you ring Pizza Hut and get them to read the menu to you? No, you wouldn't.

The whole media is a conspiracy to make us think we're no good at sex. You see sex in the films – it's totally unreal. James Bond, he sticks his arm behind his lover – does his arm go to sleep? No, it doesn't. Does his skin stick to his lover so that when he tries to move his elbow, he just rips all the skin off her back? Never happens. James Bond never had to fish six pubes out the end of his dick, did he? No! Never had to stop and say, 'Sorry, I'm going to have to fish them out love, because they're in danger of scalping me scrotum here, I'm sorry about this.' There is an absolute conspiracy to make us think that we are inadequate.

Take Kim Basinger: did you ever hear her fanny fart? No! Not once. Nine and a half weeks she was having it off. Jesus, nine and a half minutes would be a triumph for most of us. She was having it off on the ceiling, she was under the floor, she was on the bed, behind the kitchen table. Her fanny must have been so wet, the Tories must have thought about privatising it. And yet never a squelch.

BEN ELTON

Most women are wondering whether the G-spot exists. Kim
Basinger, she's got them all over her body. You've only got to tap
her on the shoulder she's having fourteen orgasms. And never a
sound. Never a sound from the nether regions. She never
greeted one of those orgasms with a great, glorious, life-
enhancing vaginal raspberry that sent her lover's dick twanging

like a Jew's harp. It's a conspiracy. Emmanuelle, she was having it off for twenty years. Never once did she gup her Spanish lover across the room. You didn't see her sheets flapping like the sails in a transatlantic race. But the rest of us, gay or straight, have to put up with the inadequacies of our bodies.

Fanny farts are a fact of heterosexual love. But it's a surprise the first time you hear one. You're making love, everything's fine, 'Oh, it's so beautiful…' [*fart noise*] '…Oh! What's that? Was that you?' 'Who, me? It wasn't fucking me! Help, there's a burglar in the room.' People are not taught what to expect. They go to therapists saying, 'Every time I have it off, there's this flatulent peeping Tom hiding in the room.' We are taught to believe that there are no juices, juices to sexuality.

Sharon Stone, she has it off in *Sliver*, she has it off in *Basic Instinct*, not a sound. And she never has to roll over into a puddle full of cold spunk, does she? Never happens. She never has the conversation with Michael Douglas about who's going to sleep in the wet patch, no. Not for Sharon Stone. But for the rest of us, we have to do it. You're making love, everything is so beautiful, then you've finished, you're rolling over, nodding off. Maybe this is a straight relationship and you think, is she asleep yet, can I risk a fart? Because you should retain some mystery in a relationship, ladies and gentlemen. A lot of lads think you've been going out for a few months, say, 'Have a whiff of that, love, what did I have for dinner?' No. It doesn't go down well, you've got to be discreet. You've got to ease it out, three or four separate sections. She says, 'I felt that.'

You wonder if she is asleep. She is not. She says, 'Get some bog paper, will you? Get lots.' You say, 'Oh bloody hell, can't it wait till morning? We'll wash the sheets on Friday.' She says, 'Get some bloody bog paper, it's all dribbling down into my bum!' [*pause*]

What, I've gone too far haven't I? I've crossed the boundary. It's a benchmark gag, that. When I was last on tour, I always knew how the audience were going to react when I done that gag.

Some towns liked it, some didn't. Edinburgh, I was nearly lynched. 'We do not have spunk in the bottom in Edinburgh, Mr Elton! It would have frozen long before it got that far.'

The thing is, you may think this is just a load of old spunk gags, but there is an important, socio-political point. Because consider our environmental politics. I'd like to be environmental, I'd like to conserve the world's resources, but on the midnight bog roll run, that's out the window. Who cares? She said, get lots. You're dragging it off the wall, the thing is spinning in its bracket, reams and reams of the stuff. Half a tree to mop up one slightly damp fanny.

IAN COGNITO

I'll tell you this: nowadays, forget the sex. I'd rather play a game of bridge, which is very similar to sex, 'cause if you haven't got a good partner, you need a good hand.

ARTHUR SMITH

I can recommend sex, it's very good for you. You know what they say: a good bit of sex is the equivalent of walking ten miles. That means some couples do up to 70,000 miles in a lifetime...and other individuals walk alone even further.

LILY SAVAGE

I had the standard Catholic sex education: nothing, fuck all. Well, that's not exactly true. My mother sat me down and she said, 'You know a man's mmm mmm' and I said 'yes' and she said, 'And you know the woman's mm mm' and I said, 'What? Own? Weekly? What?'

DISHING THE DIRT

A Short Story by Sandi Toksvig

Paul Canaille's room was plastered with his greatest triumphs and most of the triumphs were plastered with discharges from Paul Canaille. Canaille wrote the 'Dirty Stories', the muck-raking filth which sold papers, and he got off on it. Sometimes he only had to brush his hand across the headline 'Mormon Tabernacle Choir in Dwarf Sex Scandal' and he would shoot his load off there and then. He had the worst stains ever inflicted on grey serge, but he bore them like a badge of honour, for Canaille was no mere journalist. He was an artist of filth. Not for him the mere reporting of actual activity, no, Canaille made things up. He was the Hans Christian Andersen of innuendo and outrage. A man for whom the mere thought of past successes like 'Greenham Common Woman Caught with Warhead Dildo' sometimes left him incapable of walking straight for days.

But Canaille was bored. Sex that sold, sold best when the rich and famous dropped their pants and got down to it. When the chintz sofas, fresh from the family groupings in *Hello* magazine, became bonking ground for bizarre and excessive practices. But people in the public eye just weren't doing their duty and putting it about the way they used to. Canaille blamed the wretched *AIDS* business. What an annoying little disease that was. People were being careful for Christ's sake! He flicked on the telly and roamed through the channels. A besuited quiz show host was going through his paces.

'John, I believe you're a mortician in your spare time. You must have some amusing stories...'

The remote jammed in Canaille's hand as he jabbed at the 'Off' button. The wretched thing was completely useless since he'd clogged it with a particularly powerful emission over TV coverage of his story about the Irish Bishop and a transvestite missionary from Papua New Guinea. Canaille creaked up from his chair and moved towards the set. As his hand reached to terminate the tedium he suddenly knew there was a God.

Arlene Hapgood. Her face filled the screen. The soap star who'd survived the end of her soap. Who'd actually managed to make a career as an actress. A woman who had survived with dignity when she should have been reduced to opening hypermarkets and appearing on Telethons pretending to be charitable.

The announcer boomed into the room –

'Arlene Hapgood stars as Catherine the Great. A blockbusting television event bringing all the glamour, the heartache, the drama that made an ordinary girl into one of the great women of history. Arlene Hapgood is Catherine the Great.'

Arlene strutted her stuff in a chandelier-lit ballroom, swathed in brocade and pearls, batted her eyes at camera and froze into a convincingly regal vignette. After twenty years in the business she still looked like an angel. The palms of Canaille's hands began to sweat. This was the one. He was going to get her. He didn't know how, but he knew he was the man for the job.

It was one-eyed Charlie down at the Hand and Racquet who gave him the idea.

'Want a drink, Charlie?' Canaille asked as he moved to Charlie's left side, trying to avoid looking into the empty socket in the old man's head.

'Can't stop, mate,' Charlie muttered as his teeth rummaged about in his mouth. 'It's that Catherine the Great thing on tonight. I want to see if they put in the bit with the horse.' Canaille was no historian.

'Bit with the horse?'

He pulled on his lager and black.

'You know...Catherine the Great...died trying to be shafted by a horse. She had it lowered on top of her with a crane. Killed her.' Charlie winked his empty eye at Canaille. 'Wouldn't mind seeing that Arlene Hapgood take it behind from a horse.'

Canaille began to sweat. He could feel his excitement mounting as the headlines began to swim in front of him –'Arlene Hapgood in Catherine the Great Sex Romp.' No. Too intellectual. 'Arlene Hapgood Taken From Behind By Horse'. This would be the pinnacle of his career.

The Editor was less than impressed. 'Forget it, Canaille. No one will believe it. Hapgood's clean as a whistle. We've tried to get her for years.'

'But...'

'Forget it!' The Editor sorted his post into neat piles of writs, legal settlements and bills. It was going to be another week of making up the readers' letters again. 'I'll only take it if you can get pictures.'

Pictures. Bloody pictures. She was hardly likely to pose for him, was she? Or was she? Hapgood was another one of those bloody left animal lovers. A dangerous vegetarian with a mission. Canaille's mind began to work overtime, above and beyond all union regulations. First he had to sort the horse, then Ms Hapgood.

It was after the third hoisting system collapsed and broke the horse's leg that Canaille began to think of giving up. Only the thought of the massive relief the story was going to bring him kept Canaille going. Five horses and a week of rope burns and wood splinters later, he finally had the perfect horse shafting equipment. A friendly mole in the 'Animals Are Better Than Us' league had sent Hapgood a suitable invitation to lure her to the stables and Canaille was ready. He was sure she would come. She had to. He had worked so hard.

Canaille went over the plan one more time. A mickey finn in her welcoming herbal tea and under the equine erection she would go. He slapped the rump off the giant stallion and stroked the pulleys and ropes. The camera viewfinder steamed as he checked his field of vision. The horse would be raised high. Canaille pulled the huge animal into position. He would lie the actress down upon the bales of hay. Canaille lay down on his front, twisting his head to look up at the suspended creature. It was then that he heard the crack of the crumbling crane and saw half a ton of palomino approaching him at great speed. The last thing Canaille would ever recall was a searing pain in his serge and the look of a horse with a gleam in his eye.

*ONE PERSON'S FILTH CAN BE
ANOTHER DOGGIE'S POINT OF INTEREST*

filth

JOHN HEGLEY

& NIGEL

Filth!

Filth!
What my mummy called it any time I swore
Filth!
What my mummy called an agent of law
Filth!
What good boys and girls do not ask Father Christmas for.

Filth, Filth, filth, we're talking 'bout filth, Oh yes we are
Filth, filth, filth, we're talking 'bout filth la la la la la

Filth!
on the cutlery, can turn a diner off.
Filth!
but not as much as if it's floating in your broth.
Filth!
sometimes passes from my glasses to my glasses cloth,
wipey, wipey. Filth is grubby
Filth is grime
Filth is filthy
Filth doesn't rhyme
with much.

Filth, Filth, filth, we're talking about filth, oh yes we are.
Filth, filth, filth, generally unpopular.

I asked my closest friend what filthy meant to her
She said my bedroom and habits were
Filth!
it can be subjective and the subject of a jest
One person's filth can be another doggie's point of interest.

Filth, filth, filth, we're talking about filth, oh yes we are
Filth, filth, filth, occasionally, Eric Cantona
Is a filthy footballah.

John Hegley

JEREMY HARDY

One approaches the subject of filth amidst a climate of backlash really, because the right are very much trying to undo the damage done by the permissive Sixties and I have to say that I can remember the Sixties and they weren't that permissive; apart from being allowed to stay up for 'High Chaperal' on a Monday night – that was about it.

MARK THOMAS

Filth is the theme of the show. I'll tell you what I think filth is, and this is my definition of filth. There was a politician called Nicholas Ridley who actually said there was no such thing as rape. And that's filth. Because if you believe that then you must believe that every single woman in the world walks around every waking moment of her life actively looking for sex from any man whatsoever. If that was the case, men would not go out, we'd live in fear of our fucking lives. We'd just be looking out behind the curtains. 'Is it safe?' 'Yeah. Go!' 'Fuck, I've got one on my leg. GEDDOFF!' Women would spend all their time hanging out on building sites: 'You're the only ones that understand us.' That's filth.

IAN COGNITO

The sun was out today, and the only bad thing about that is it means the fucking windscreen cleaners are out – 'the beggars with the bucket', I call them. Last season, though, last fucking windscreen cleaning season I got one; he was bobbing about down the bottom of my road. I put my boot down and I fuck-ing hit him (I've got an Astra so I don't give a fuck what happens to it). I've gone Bang, I've gone over his plastic bucket and sent it flying. I've gone over his sponge and given it a right good wringing out. And I've hit him on the way through.

But I've reversed up, right, and I said to him, 'Sorry about that, mate, I never saw you there...my windscreen's filthy. Bye.'

AN COGNITO

I read *The Dice Man* by Luke Reinhart, it's a great book. I read it about a month ago and I defy anyone to read the book and not fucking do it at the end of the night, not actually roll the dice and have six options of things you're going to do and go, 'Fuck it, I'm going to do it if it comes up.' And I did it and I'll tell you what my six options were:

Option number one. If number one came up on the dice I was going to have a nice cup of Earl Grey Tea and a whole packet of cup cakes.

Option two. If two came up on the dice I was going to go up the pub, spend all my money on Guinness and Glenfiddich.

If number three came up on the dice I was going to look at the pile of videos crawling up the corner of the room and have a nice fat spliff.

If number four came up on the dice I was going to lock the bathroom door, grease myself up with the Oil of Ulay and have a bloody good J. Arthur.

If option five came up – I was going to do exactly the same as option number four.

If option number six came upon the dice I was going to agree to do that charity gig 'Filth' that's full of TV stars and where your name's not even on the fucking front cover of the book!!

ARTHUR SMITH

London is really getting me down these days. It's filthy, nothing works, there's dog shit everywhere, none of it's white, and that's just my flat.

I called in a builder the other day to give me a quote and he said, 'Do not forsake me, oh my darling.' I said, 'You're a bloody cowboy, mate, aren't you?'

But you know what they say – when a man is tired of London, he's tired of life; when a man is tired of Swindon, he's been there about ten minutes. Don't ever go there. Honestly, it's a ghastly place. It's twinned with a mud flat in Siberia.

I went to the tourist office in Swindon and said, 'Excuse me, can you point out anywhere round here that isn't shit and boring?' and she said, 'Well, have you tried the industrial estate around the corner?' And I said, 'Are you taking the piss?' and she said, 'Well, you started it.'

And I entered a marathon the other day. That was terrible. Chocolate and peanuts all over my knob. That joke doesn't really work now. We don't even call them Marathons any more; there's a conspiracy among the chocolate companies. It doesn't sound the same – 'I entered a Snickers the other day', just not quite the same laugh at all.

A couple of questions. Why is it, do you think, that there are enough traffic cones for every student in Britain to have one in their bedroom?

And secondly, and this is the question that's perplexing me amongst all the problems of the world; whatever happened, *whatever* happened, to white dog shit?

Because there always used to be white dog shit, didn't there? When you were a kid, you'd be walking along and it'd be, 'Oh, there's a bit of white dog shit there, there's another bit there and another bit there.' You could see up to about thirty or forty bits of white dog shit in a day. 'I might have a nibble at that bit there.' The only white dog shit you see these days: Leeds United.

Not a gag I would tell in Leeds, I hasten to add. I was up in Leeds recently and a bloke said to me, 'Hey you, you, where are you from?' 'I'm from London,' I said. 'No you're not,' he said, 'you're a cockney, bastard twat! What are you?' And you know, he was quite a big bloke, and frankly, I could see his point of view. I had to concede that I was indeed, a cockney bastard twat.

He said, 'Do you reckon you're a comedian? I tell you what, I'll tell you the bloody best joke in the world.' I said, 'Well, go on then,' and he said, 'What did the Yorkshireman say to the Londoner?' I said, 'I don't know, what did the Yorkshireman say to the Londoner?' He said, 'Fuck off back to London, you cockney bastard twat.' And the curious thing was that I went up on stage and said that, and indeed it was the best joke in the world. They absolutely loved it.

LILY SAVAGE

Well, they rang me up and they said, 'Lily, we want you to come on and talk about sex and be absolutely filthy,' and I said, 'Well, as the general secretary of the Union of Catholic Mothers, Wirral branch, I don't feel inclined to do that, especially on a stage where Dame Margot Fonteyn and Postman Pat have walked.' I thought, no, I can't.

I'll tell you what is fucking filthy, though – when it's windy and you're walking behind a fella in the street (and it's always fellas who do this), and they go [*hawking noise as Lily gathers up phlegm in throat and mimes gobbing*], and it all flies back and it's hanging off the hood of your anorak.

Or they go 'Phnnnn' [*Lily puts finger on one nostril and blows out of the other*], and it hits the wheel of your shopping trolley going round Sainsbury's like a bloody snail leaving tracks.

And why do fellas wipe their dicks on the duvet when they've had a shag? That really pisses me off. Little crusty bits. I blamed the cats.

My cats, one of them was on heat, she's just come off, the other one's come on now. Fucking screaming five o'clock in the morning. 'Waaaaaaaaah! [*cat screaming noise*] Yes, we'd all like a shag, but we're not dragging our arses on the cork flooring, get to sleep!'

I'm sitting on the couch trying to eat my dinner and they come in, backside first, this hole like a white-knuckle ride at Alton Towers. Your sausage is sucked off the plate, all the peas go individually, your spuds fly off, you're hanging off the arm of the couch, your flip-flops are beating the fuck off the soles of your feet, the curtains are stiff. Jesus Christ!

And when they get on your knee [*very loud purr*], all your fillings are being moved. The neighbours thought it was me, and I was embarrassed. So I'd had enough this night because I was angst, because I'm not on the valium any more – they took me off it and the halcyon, the bastards. I want Prozac but they won't give it me.

So I got up and put a rubber glove on, and I don't recommend this for anybody at home, a marigold full-length evening glove, and went in the kitchen and they're there, writhing by the bin [*deep purr*]. And I went 'Shut up.' [*Mimes sticking finger up cat.*] How do you explain in casualty, five o'clock in the morning, a Persian cat hanging off the end of your hand? Should have seen me getting on the bus – I had to pretend it was me handbag.

JULIAN CLARY

I feel a bit of a fool actually. I've got very bad handwriting and I looked in my diary this morning and I seem to have written 'Felch benefit'. Not very right on, is it?

Still, I thought I'd better turn up. Thought I was coming to some kind of felching convention. Brought my own straw with me. But it won't be necessary. Oh, there's a selection of men down here in the orchestra pits. How thoughtful. Hello. It's like the back bar at Substation.

Funny place, that. I don't know if you've ever been in it. There's a nightclub policy there – you're not allowed to leave until you've picked up some old dog. I met somebody there with a brown hanky and a spoon in his top pocket...and he wasn't one of the Bisto Kids either. They asked for filth, and I thought I'd oblige.

Steve Bell

Steve Bell

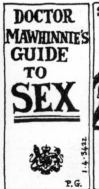

Steve Bell

Steve Bell

filth!
THE VIDEO
filth!
Safe Sex Dangerous Comedy

18

WARNING:

The most outrageous comedy event of the century

An exclusive viewing of comic material un-transmittable on television

Available Now From All Good Video Stores
srp £12.99

PICKWICK